Royal Doulton

Royal Doulton

Jennifer Quérée

ROBERT HALE • LONDON

First published in Great Britain 1993

ISBN 0-7090-5180-8

Robert Hale Limited
Clerkenwell House
Clerkenwell Green
London EC1R OHT

Printed in Korea

Contents

Author's Note

*I*n 1971 a now legendary exhibition of Doulton Lambeth stonewares was organized in London by Richard Dennis. In the reaction against the decorative arts of the Victorian era the products of the Doulton Studios, as with many other ceramics of the period, had for many years been dismissed as "misapplied art". Few collectors and students of ceramics were aware of the extent and excellence of the Doulton range of products and the extraordinary variety of bodies, processes and decorative techniques which had been employed. To many the 1971 exhibition was a revelation.

That it proved an inspiration also is witnessed world-wide by the explosion of interest in Doulton wares from that date to the present. People looked at Doulton family heirlooms with renewed interest. Antique shops and attics alike were combed for anything bearing a Doulton backstamp. Royal Doulton itself recognized the value of encouraging this trend, and established an International Collectors' Club.

Three major exhibitions have followed since 1971 – two in London (1975 and 1979), and one in Sydney (also 1979). The intention of the 1992-3 New Zealand Exhibition was to concentrate on the Doulton decorative wares, principally covering the period 1869-1939, but including additional examples of very early and more recent or "in production" pieces. Such an exhibition was envisaged as appealing not only to Doulton collectors, but also to china painters, potters, students of ceramic history, and to the many people who were familiar from childhood with at least one item of Doulton – whether it was a "Bunnykins" porridge bowl, a "Gaffers" plate, or an "Old Balloon Seller" figurine. In fact, such is the variety of Doulton ceramic products over the years, that here was one exhibition which could with confidence be seen as having "something for everyone, young or old".

Publicity about the proposed touring exhibition rapidly generated enormous enthusiasm. Generous offers of loan material were received from museums and, in particular, private individuals, across the country and from Australia and the United Kingdom. In 1991 Canterbury Museum joined the National Art Gallery and Museum (now the Museum of New Zealand Te Papa Tongarewa) in the preparation and curation of the Doulton Exhibition. Major sponsorship from CourierPost (New Zealand Post Ltd.) solved the logistical headache of transporting such a massive, fragile and valuable collection throughout New Zealand. In addition, publicity was greatly enhanced by New Zealand Post's decision to have a major stamp issue using some of the Doulton ceramics from the exhibition. It is believed that this is the first time Royal Doulton wares have been so featured, and these stamps are sure to become collectors' items. Together with CourierPost,

Television New Zealand helped with the nationwide promotion of the exhibition.

Any author writing about Doulton is heavily indebted to the late Desmond Eyles, for many years Publicity Officer, researcher and unofficial archivist for Royal Doulton. I wish particularly to acknowledge *The Doulton Lambeth Wares* (1975), now (sadly) out of print, and *The Doulton Burslem Wares* (1980). Both books have been a source of otherwise inaccessible information. Edmund Gosse, Sir Henry Doulton's official biographer, likewise provided invaluable personal and historic insights into both the man and the firm.

Acknowledgment must also be made to the following:

Royal Doulton (U.K.) Ltd for research and exhibition support.

CourierPost (N.Z.) Ltd as principal sponsors for the exhibition.

James Mack and David Harcourt, who initiated the exhibition.

The many collectors who generously offered hospitality, shared their knowledge, or lent to the exhibition, in particular: Geoffrey Bell, Norma and Maurice Boylson, Nancy and Bill Coupland, Alma and Les Foster, Judith Johnson, Jocelyn Lukins, Colin and Susan Payne, Doug and Joy Redmond, John Shorter C.B.E. and Keith and Doris Smith.

The staff of Museums and Art Galleries which hold collections of Doulton: **Art Gallery of New South Wales, Sydney**; **Auckland Museum**; **Canterbury Museum, Christchurch** (in particular: Jenny Barton, Sheila Lewthwaite, Beverley McCulloch, Deborah Roil, Robin Sutton, Richard Taylor, Michael Trotter); **City Museum and Art Gallery, Stoke-on-Trent** (in particular: Pat Halfpenny); **Dunedin Public Art Gallery**; **Hawkes Bay Cultural Trust and Museum, Napier**; **Manawatu Museum**; **Otago Museum**; **Minet Library, Lambeth**; **Museum of Applied Arts and Sciences, Sydney** (in particular: Eva Czernis-Ryl, Jai Paterson, Goscia Dudek); **Museum of Garden History, Lambeth**; **Museum of London** (in particular: Jane Zeuner, Kay Staniland); **Museum of New Zealand Te Papa Tongarewa, Wellington** (in particular: Alan Baker, Jenny Harper, Fritha Marriage, Raewyn Smith, Pat Stuart); **Sir Henry Doulton Gallery, Burslem** (in particular: Valerie Baynton); **Victoria and Albert Museum, London**.

Margaret Taylor, and Richard Taylor, who travelled the country collecting and packing, and who kept my enthusiasm from waning.

Gillian Wess (Bookhouse Publishing Ltd.), Walter Cook, and Ron Lambert for assistance in publishing.

Special thanks to friends and family, for encouragement and support over the three years of exhibition preparation and time spent on this book.

Photographers: Warren Jacobs and Steve Goodenough (Canterbury Museum photographs); Chris Matthews (Hawkes Bay Cultural Trust photographs); Norman Heke (Museum of New Zealand Te Papa Tongarewa photographs); Ray Woodbury (Art Gallery of New South Wales photographs).

Published with the assistance of the **Winifred Swires Bequest Fund (Canterbury Museum)**.

Royal Doulton – the New Zealand Story

*I*t has been estimated that two out of three New Zealand households contain at least one Doulton product – be it in the bathroom, the china cabinet, on the wall, or used at the dinner table. Many New Zealanders ate their first meal from a Bunnykins plate. Parents and grandparents had living rooms decorated with Royal Doulton's "Fair Ladies", or quaint rack plates which perhaps illustrated characters from the familiar tales of Charles Dickens, or showed funny old English countrymen in smocks. Over the years the quirky character jugs have been firm favourites for gifts, which may then have formed the foundation for a collection. Royal Doulton tableware has always been highly regarded and can be found in all sorts of places; today, those who fly Business Class on New Zealand airlines will find their refreshments served on it.

New Zealand museums contain excellent examples of Doulton ceramics both utilitarian and decorative, but by far the greatest number and variety of wares are found in private collections. Some – the fortunate few – have inherited, or happened upon, stunning examples of Doulton's art ceramics – elaborately decorated stonewares from Lambeth, sumptuous hand-painted or richly-glazed pieces from Burslem.

The New Zealand architectural landscape, too, is littered with Doulton wares, although it is probable that these are not so readily identified as such by the passing public. In Christchurch, the Victorian warehouses in Lichfield Street have doorways with patented Doulton tiles. The grand foyer of the Dunedin Railway Station, opened in 1907, is splendidly embellished with Renaissance-style faience mouldings, tiles and a mosaic floor from Doulton's Lambeth works.

In 1912 a set of Doulton nursery rhyme tiles was imported for use in the Wellington Children's Hospital. They were rescued from demolition in 1989, as was a similar set in the Children's Ward of Christchurch Public Hospital in 1990. Both tile schemes are to be restored and reinstated in new buildings.

The War Memorial Hall, Mount Eden, houses a large circular directional table, showing a map of the Auckland isthmus and the distances to a host of New Zealand and overseas towns and cities. Originally sited on the top of Mt Eden, it was commissioned from Royal Doulton in 1928 by Sir Ernest Davis, local politician and philanthropist.

More than 19 000 kilometres from their point of origin, Doulton ceramics could be said to be a household name, but where and when did New Zealand's patronage of Royal Doulton begin?

Much of the evidence seems to point very strongly to Canterbury, in the South Island, and in particular to the once-famous china shop

A Doulton Lambeth stand which shows Chiné Ware (Doulton & Slater's Patent), Natural Foliage (Repousée) Ware, and what was probably the first showing of Maori Ware, at the John Bates & Co. pavilion, N.Z.I.E., Christchurch, 1906.

The Royal Doulton showroom at John Bates & Co., Worcester House, Christchurch, c. 1926.

of John Bates & Co. Ltd. of Christchurch. John William Bates was born in Derbyshire in 1860 and emigrated to Dunedin with his parents in 1873. Some time later he joined the china and glass firm of Matheson Bros., who sent him to take charge of their newly-opened branch in Christchurch. In 1879, at the age of 19, Bates started in business on his own account, initially in partnership with R. L. McLenaghen. In June 1883 the partnership was dissolved and henceforth the business was known as John Bates & Co., trading as "Worcester House" at 118-120 Cashel Street.

Over the years Bates developed an immense knowledge of, and genuine love for, the fine ceramics and glass in which he dealt. This was passed on to his many customers, a number of whom, under his guidance, formed the exceptionally fine collections still in their families' possession today. The quality of Bates & Co.'s merchandise – down to its final days under the third generation of family ownership in the early 1970s – was such that the firm never had to advertise commercially, but could rely on word of mouth. It was not uncommon for North Island visitors attending Race Week in Christchurch to bring down substantial sums of money for the sole purpose of purchasing fine china at Bates'.

It would seem that small quantities of the "art pottery" from Doulton's Lambeth Studio had made its way to find a limited market in late 19th century New Zealand. Photographs of the period reveal some Lambeth stonewares amongst Japanese and European ceramics, suggesting that they appealed to the more avant-garde colonist. On the whole, however, it was Worcester, Derby, Coalport, Minton, or Copeland, from which the comfortably-situated colonist sought decorative ceramics for the home. (In Australia, and particularly in Sydney, the Doulton Wares, including such products as Lambeth Faience, were more abundant, particularly after the publicity generated by the 1879 International Exhibition in Sydney.)

However, in 1906 Royal Doulton took New Zealand by storm, to establish a market which has remained faithful ever since. In that year, the advent of the New Zealand International Exhibition of Art and Industry in Christchurch exposed the public to an unprecedented array of Doulton's art ceramics. The *Official Record* of the Exhibition described:

> ... the particularly beautiful displays, setting quite a new standard to New Zealand people in high-class art pottery. Finest of all was the splendid collection of Doulton ware [exhibited by J. Bates & Co.], including many vases and bowls of beautiful pattern; some of these, masterpieces of the designer's and potter's arts, were priced as high as £500 each.

The British Government Arts and Crafts Section also included examples of the latest Doulton art wares. Most were quickly purchased by enthusiastic ceramics collectors. *The Press* of Christchurch, 23 March 1907, recorded:

John Bates & Co.'s pavilion at the New Zealand International Exhibition of Art and Industry [N.Z.I.E.], Christchurch, in 1906, with the first major display of Royal Doulton ceramics to be shown in New Zealand.

Exhibits at the John Bates & Co. pavilion, N.Z.I.E., Christchurch, 1906. Hand-painted Burslem ceramics by Leslie Johnson, George Buttle, Harry Piper and Robert Allen,

The Royal Doulton wares from John Bates & Co's stand at the N.Z.I.E. received a record number of gold medals and special awards. The announcement in *The Press*, Christchurch, was reprinted as a publicity pamphlet by Bates.

It is a noteworthy fact that the exhibits of Messrs Doulton and Co. were considered of sufficient importance to merit the bestowal of three special awards and eighteen gold medals, which constitutes a record, as the greatest number of highest awards ever granted for an exhibit of Ceramic Art at any Exposition in the world.

Later exhibitions – the Auckland Exhibition in 1913 and the New Zealand and South Seas Exhibition in Dunedin in 1925 – saw additional large displays of Doulton wares by Bates and other major retailers such as Tanfield Potter of Auckland. These businessmen were in regular contact with the Doulton works, either directly or through the Australasian agency of John Shorter & Co. of Sydney.

John Shorter had been appointed as Doulton's official distributor in Australia in 1892, in order to consolidate its position in a market established in 1879 at the time of the Sydney International Exhibition. For three generations Shorter & Co. imported industrial and domestic Doulton wares into Australia, and ensured that New Zealand had an equally wide choice. John Bates dealt directly with the Doulton factories, but nevertheless had a long-standing and harmonious relationship with the Shorter firm and family.

Preparations for the 1992-3 New Zealand Exhibition of Royal Doulton Ceramics revealed that a number of pieces acquired at the 1906 Exhibition or later, through Bates and others, were still in New Zealand, in the possession of either the original purchasers' families or modern collectors. Through the early close contacts between Bates and Shorter, some had found their way back to Sydney and several can be located amongst the magnificent Doulton collection of the Museum of Applied Arts and Sciences (the Powerhouse Museum). Where possible all such pieces were included in the Exhibition.

The New Zealand and Australian collections are particularly strong in Burslem hand-painted items of the highest quality, as well as stunning examples of Flambé, Sung, Chang, Titanian, Crystalline and Rembrandt Wares. These were the latest and most exciting products of the Burslem factory in the early years of the twentieth century, and were quickly snapped up by Shorter and Bates.

Wealthy New Zealand runholders, sheep-breeders, politicians and city merchants, eager to furnish their large houses with objects of beauty and conspicuous quality, succumbed to the blandishments of John Bates and his stock of vases, plates and even tea-sets by Edward Raby, George White, John Hugh Plant and Leslie Johnson. Some, connoisseurs of Oriental ceramics, were intrigued and astounded by the achievements in Flambé and even Chang (although the latter was notoriously difficult stock to "shift", being rather in advance of its time).

Bates' display at the 1906 Exhibition had also included a number of the earlier Lambeth products of Hannah and Florence Barlow, some

Lambeth Doulton Wares by Hannah Barlow and Mark V. Marshall, at the John Bates & Co. pavilion, N.Z.I.E., Christchurch, 1906.

The drawing room of a wealthy collector's house in Christchurch in the early 1930s. The owner was a colonial success story, having made his money from breeding merino sheep. He spent it on fine paintings, glass, furniture and ceramics, including Royal Doulton. Many of the ceramics were acquired through John Bates.

A group of vases by George White at the John Bates & Co. pavilion, N.Z.I.E., Christchurch, 1906. The plate bears a portrait, painted from a photograph, of John Bates' daughter.

vellum figures of the 1890s, George Tinworth religious plaques, enamelled panels by Noke, and a tile scheme by Margaret Thompson (*The Fairies at the Christening*). Nearly all of these won gold medals or special awards, illustrating as they did some of the best pieces by the major Lambeth artists.

A quantity of Chiné and Natural Foliage Ware pieces were also shown as were early versions of the Kia Ora or Maori decorated stonewares. The latter were the first in a range of wares – never large, and of somewhat parochial appeal – with a special New Zealand flavour.

Following the 1906 Exhibition, and up until the early 1940s, Bates – and other china specialists – continued to stock Doulton products in quantity. The figures and animals produced from 1913 onwards had universal appeal, while a vast range of Series wares (available from the earlier 1900s), was within reach of all who cared to buy. Every year Bates & Co. sent extensive orders to the potteries for these, as well as the more luxury products such as the Flambés and hand-painted items, together with vast quantities of table and other utilitarian wares.

Following the Second World War, production of much of the Doulton decorative wares had ceased. The power, beauty and technical brilliance of the early 20th century Burslem transmutation glazes was soon forgotten. Hand-painted Burslem and Lambeth stoneware wares were (to modern "minimalist" eyes) over-decorated and vulgar. Serious connoisseurs, students of ceramics, and the newly-rich – for whom the antique markets and salerooms were accessible in a way not possible for their colonial grandparents – were not much

A group of hand-painted Royal Doulton Burslem vases by Edward Raby. The spectacular "Alexandra" vase (centre), 142 cm tall, was considered one of the highlights of the Exhibition. It is still in existence.

Doulton Lambeth ceramics by Margaret E. Thompson [*The Fairies at the Christening* – removed from New Zealand and now in the United Kingdom], Francis Pope and Frank A. Butler, at the John Bates & Co. pavilion, N.Z.I.E., Christchurch, 1906.

A group of hand-painted pieces by David Dewsberry at the John Bates & Co. pavilion, N.Z.I.E., Christchurch, 1906.

interested in anything made after 1840. In the 1950s and 1960s New Zealand studio pottery was beginning to blossom, and the strongest influence was that of Japanese potters such as Hamada, working in a folk tradition. "Commercial" ceramics were greeted by many with a sneer.

Royal Doulton no longer produced Series Ware in any great quantity or variety. For some years it fell out of favour, regarded as merely old-fashioned without the distinction of being "antique". Character jugs and figurines, however, were (and are) still in production and continued to enjoy a significant degree of popularity.

Ironically, perhaps it was an increased knowledge brought about by the actual experience of throwing and decorating pots, particu-

Doulton Lambeth ceramics by George Tinworth, Florence Barlow and Elise [Eliza] Simmance at the John Bates & Co. pavilion, N.Z.I.E., Christchurch, 1906.

larly in stoneware, which eventually opened some New Zealanders' eyes to the quality of the earlier Doulton wares. A hugely-popular vogue for china painting also led that group to an early appreciation of the talents of the Burslem artists.

The inevitable swing of the pendulum in fine and decorative art appreciation ultimately resulted in a reassessment, in New Zealand as elsewhere, of the virtues as well as the failings of the Victorian and early 20th century period. The place of the undeniably-commercial firm of Royal Doulton in the European and English ceramic arts tradition is now well-established, with wide recognition of the skill of its designers, artists, chemists and technicians. Few museums today would deny that, ceramic qualities aside, the Doulton wares provide an almost-perfect mirror of changing popular taste in decorative domestic arts, from the 1860s to the present.

And, of course, there have always been those for whom the variable winds of fashion or scholarship mean little. In simply enjoying their Doulton vase, figurine, rack plate, or character jug, they would no doubt heartily agree with Henry Doulton's own words:

> There is a great deal of dogmatism on what is and what is not fine art. In art there are many mansions ...

The Waterside Pottery

W hat is the "Doulton story" and where does the "art pottery" fit in? What was the philosophy which lay behind the product? Who were the people producing these engaging and remarkable ceramics? As with many enterprises the origins were humble.

In 1815, in London's parish of Lambeth on the south bank of the Thames, a young man invested his life's savings of £100 in a small pottery business. It was only one of some 174 potteries in London, but in the years which have since elapsed, virtually all the others have disappeared, while it has survived to become one of the famous names in English ceramic history.

The young potter was John Doulton. He had received his training at the historic Fulham Pottery, often referred to as the "cradle of English ceramics". After working for three years at the Vauxhall Walk establishment of Mrs Martha Jones, John was taken into partnership together with the foreman, John Watts. In 1820 Mrs Jones retired and the firm became "Doulton and Watts", the total staff comprising the two partners, another thrower and an apprentice.

The business turned out quantities of practical objects: ink and blacking bottles, beetle traps, flasks and tankards for ale, tobacco jars and soap containers, paint jars, chimney pots and garden vases, and, eventually, condensing worms, retorts, acid pumps, taps and large storage containers for the chemical industries. The ever-increasing populations of London and the industrial cities had led to dangerous pollution of their water supplies, and water filters for home use were in great demand.

"Fancy wares" were also produced. These included Toby Jugs – not the Staffordshire figural type in the form of a man holding a foaming tankard, but the tankard itself, rim and handle dipped in a darker slip glaze and the body covered with applied moulded sprigs of windmills, trees, and hunting and drinking scenes. These, and other utensils decorated with the same sprigs, remained in production for 150 years. Other popular wares were spirit flasks, either in the shape of well-known politicians such as Lord Brougham, or depicting characters popularised in the new satirical magazine, *Punch*.

Enter Henry Doulton

John Doulton's second son, Henry, was a sensitive and intelligent boy, whose abilities seemed to point to a university career, the law or the church. Somewhat to his family's surprise, however, Henry was determined to become a practising potter and man of business like his father. Thus, in 1835 at the age of 15, he started work in the pottery, preparing and throwing the clay and learning all aspects of the craft. At night he continued his studies – technical drawing, chemistry,

Salt-glazed moulded stoneware spirit flask, *The Triumph of the Pen*, 1850s. The scenes were adapted from a cartoon in *Punch* magazine. Doulton & Watts, Lambeth. Height 18 cm.
Collection: Museum of Applied Arts and Sciences, Sydney, Australia.

Henry Doulton in 1861, from a portrait by Frederick Sandys.

Salt-glazed stoneware water filter case, two gallon capacity. Doulton & Watts, Lambeth, 1850s. Height 38 cm.
Private Collection

physics, metallurgy, history, literature, and poetry, for which he developed a particular love.

A Fortune Down the Drain

In addition to polluted drinking water, an almost complete lack of proper sanitation and drainage in the expanding cities of the early 19th century had resulted in horrifying epidemics of cholera and typhoid. Lambeth itself was described, in a poster of 1832, as a:

> ... Pest-House of the Metropolis, and a disgrace to the Nation, [in which] the main thoroughfares are still without Common Sewers, although the Inhabitants have paid exorbitant Rates from time immemorial!!!

By the 1840s it was realised that underground sewerage and drainage, using salt-glazed stoneware pipes (rather than wooden or porous earthenware ones), was the answer to this problem. Henry Doulton – a shrewd and ambitious young businessman – anticipated that a sanitation revolution was about to take place, and that any firm in a position to satisfy the demand for appropriate wares would make a great deal of money. John Doulton was at first less than enthusiastic about undertaking such a project, so in 1846 Henry formed his own company, renting premises in Lambeth High Street to establish the first English factory devoted to the exclusive production of stoneware pipes.

Henry Doulton was nothing if not up to date, and quickly installed recently-patented machinery for extruding pipes in one piece. Doulton conduits and pipes were soon vanishing beneath the buildings and streets of London and the other great cities of Britain, and in a relatively short time further Doulton factories were set up in Lancashire and Worcestershire to cope with the demand. Watts retired in 1853, and in 1854 the firms of Doulton and Watts and Henry Doulton and Company amalgamated to form Doulton and Company. Many of the drainage and sewer pipes produced by these factories more than a hundred years ago are still functioning today, in places as far flung as Russia, South America and Australia.

Such indispensable but unattractive objects may seem to have little connection with the majority of Doulton wares commonly found in living rooms or in museums of applied arts today. However, without the sewer pipes it is doubtful whether there would have been the finance, the experience or the reputation for quality necessary to launch into the fields of "art" pottery or fine ceramics.

A New Venture

By the mid-1860s Henry Doulton was making a comfortable fortune, and was more inclined to follow literary and political pursuits than start any new potting ventures. For some years he had been pestered by the Head of the recently-formed Lambeth School of Art, John Sparkes, to employ some of his students. They were to gain practical design experience in an industrial environment, and to produce

Salt-glazed stoneware Hunting Ware jug with a silver rim, 1903. Royal Doulton, Lambeth. Height 14.3 cm.
Canterbury Museum Collection.

objects which were at the same time utilitarian and artistic. Eventually, in 1866, Doulton was reluctantly persuaded to admit one particularly talented young man, George Tinworth. Poor George was consigned to a corner of the factory, given a chimney pot on which to sit, a tub to balance a modelling board on, and told that he could use only the clays, glazes and kilns utilized for the pipes. Initially he designed some water filter cases and modelled a number of large terra-cotta medallions in a neo-classical style. The latter impressed the art critic John Ruskin, who later did much to bring Tinworth to the attention of the art world.

Tinworth also began designing and decorating stoneware vases and jugs which were thrown by one of the factory's potters. These he etched with a piece of pointed boxwood while they were still in the soft state. Although the forms were inspired by the historic stonewares of Cologne, Germany, Tinworth's decorative motifs were quite original and became increasingly characteristic – seaweed-like trails, scrolls and leafy forms, with raised bosses and beaded runners. Unlike the rather cold blue- or grey-bodied German stonewares, the Doulton pots were generally a warm brown or beige colour, mainly due to different firing methods and the use of coal rather than wood as a fuel. Experiments were carried out at the factory and the Lambeth School of Art in adding colours (blue and brown) to the simple wares.

These early pots had to take their chance in the kilns with the pipes and, because of the lack of control during the days-long firing process, the early results were frequently disappointing, with the colours running or fleeing altogether. Nevertheless, in 1867 Henry Doulton agreed to the exhibition of a selection of these early studio wares at the Paris Exhibition. The 30 pots met with modest success, French

Self-portrait medallion of press-moulded terracotta, by George Tinworth, c. 1895. Height 15.5 cm.
Collection: Museum of Applied Arts and Sciences, Sydney, Australia.

Left: Salt-glazed and incised stoneware spill vase, with applied beading and two moulded mice, by George Tinworth assisted by Emma A. Burrows, 1881. Doulton & Co., Lambeth. Height 13.5 cm. *Manawatu Museum Society (Inc.) Collection.*
Right: Salt-glazed stoneware lemonade jug with a silver rim, carved, coloured and beaded decoration by George Tinworth assisted by Fanny Clark, 1881. Doulton & Co., Lambeth. Height 24 cm. *Private Collection.*

critics predicting a new and interesting development in English art ceramics.

Thus encouraged, John Sparkes wheedled Henry Doulton into setting up a small "art department" at the pottery. The objective was to produce a range of wares for the forthcoming International Exhibition at South Kensington in 1871. Tinworth was responsible for most of the pots produced, but a small number were created by four students from the Lambeth School of Art. The latter included Hannah Barlow (who had had some experience at Minton's Art Pottery Studio in London) and her talented brother, Arthur.

To Henry Doulton's immense surprise the wares were greeted with great enthusiasm. Spotted by Mr Sodden Smith, a member of the Exhibition Committee, they were rescued from obscurity in a dark corner, and placed in a prominent position adjacent to cases containing the work of such famous art potteries as Wedgwood, Minton and Spode. The contrast to the somewhat fussy approach of these factories, which were above all concerned with surface decoration, was refreshing. Here was robust English pottery straight from the hands of the craftsman, full of simple vitality, made to be handled and loved. All but six of the batch of some 70 pieces were snapped up by public and connoisseurs alike. One of the purchasers was Queen Victoria, who ordered some to be sent up to Windsor – thus beginning a long and still-standing patronage of the firm by British royalty.

Salt-glazed, incised stoneware jug, by Arthur Barlow, 1871-2, illustrating some of the colouring problems of the early kiln firings. Doulton & Co., Lambeth. Height 14.1 cm. *Auckland Museum Collection.*

Doulton Wares – Art Pottery at Lambeth

*H*enry Doulton owed his commercial success to the ability to comprehend and grasp an opportunity when it arose. He was by now enthusiastic about this new product, convinced that it had not only artistic merit but a degree of commercial viability. In fact, it never really paid its way, but the prestige and world-wide publicity which the art wares soon brought to Doulton was beyond price.

With money to spare from the pipe works and industrial products Henry set about to add to his staff, and build proper art studios and workshops in the newly-enlarged premises in Lambeth High Street. Tinworth was joined full time in 1871-2 by Hannah and Arthur Barlow, Emily Edwards and Frank Butler. In 1873 the ranks were swelled by nine more, including Florence Barlow, Eliza Simmance, Arthur Pearce and John Broad. By 1881, 249 designers, artists and assistants were employed, 229 of whom were women.

Henry Doulton's attitudes to female emancipation and employment make interesting reading today, when many countries of the Western World accept (in principle at least) the notion of female suffrage and equal opportunities for women. In an address in the 1880s, Doulton said:

> I am not one of those who are disposed to join in the agitation for what are called 'women's rights', but I have a strong love and admiration for women, and I believe that their power and influence are far above those of our own sex …The true sphere of women is the family and the household, and I believe that the contact of women with the strifes and rivalries in which public men are involved would weaken that beneficent influence which they exert over our sex. The great problem as to female employment presents many difficulties, but I am exceedingly happy in the knowledge that the faltering steps I took some ten years ago have led to so complete and satisfactory a solution of this question. Probably I had some prejudices in regard to women's work …In Staffordshire I have seen women and young girls employed in the most coarse and degrading labour, such as turning the wheels, wedging the clay, etc. I always declined to employ female labour in the ordinary work of the factory, and it was not until Mr Rix had placed before me a well-organised scheme that I agreed to employ girls and women in our art department. I still feel that women's work should be as far as possible restricted to occupations not involving severe labour, and as much as practicable to the Arts that beautify and adorn life.

When Henry Doulton was awarded the Albert Medal of the (Royal) Society of Arts in 1885, for "… the great impulse given…to the production of art pottery…", particular recognition was made of the "… services rendered by Mr Doulton to the cause of technical education, especially the technical education of women …"

Silicon Ware water filter with moulded and hand-applied sprigs. Doulton & Co., Lambeth 1885. The artist who designed this filter for reproduction is unknown, but the assistants were Laura Green, Kate E. Russell, Florence Bowditch, Ada Mayerek and Eborah Bissmire.
Walter C. Cook Decorative Art Collection, Museum of New Zealand Te Papa Tongarewa.

"The Leisure Hour" 1885, "Girls come to the pottery at an early age, before they have lost that digital suppleness so essential to all delicate handicrafts, and most necessary to the work of shaping and moulding the pliant and tender clay."

Female (and male) employees were able to work their way up from probationer to assistant to acknowledged artist, each work day concluding with classes at the Lambeth School of Art. For their inspiration and guidance Doulton furnished a small museum with pottery from ancient Greece and Rome, and a range of ceramics from all the best traditional European centres. This was complemented by a library of art books, a music room, recreation area and a dining hall. In an illuminated address presented to Henry Doulton in 1881 (now in the possession of the Minet Library, Lambeth), the "Lady Artists and Assistants" made their gratitude plain:

> We ... desire to take this opportunity of expressing our obligations to you for the origination of an occupation at once interesting and elevating to so large a number of our sex. We also desire to record our very high appreciation of the arrangements made for our comfort and convenience in the various sections.

Notwithstanding his admitted prejudices and (by today's standards, at least) paternalistic attitude, Henry Doulton undoubtedly did further the cause of "women's rights" in England, by providing equal opportunities for work-related education as well as the means of earning a respectable living with good conditions and fair pay.

Production Techniques

A distinguishing characteristic of the Doulton Wares, as they became known, was their having been thrown on the potter's wheel. A contemporary critic, writing in *The Times*, commented on:

> ... the contrast which they offer to the somewhat namby-pamby prettiness, cast out of moulds by the gross and painted in strict adherence to a copy, which form the bulk of what is generally known as ornamental porcelain ... Everything is the direct result of the mind and the hand of the workman or of the artist.

While several of the artists had some experience of actual potting, their usual method was to design on paper or model in miniature the desired shape which they intended to decorate. These were then produced by experienced throwers, some of whom on occasion also submitted their own designs. Always there was the highest degree of collaboration between artist-designer and potter.

Most of the pots, whilst in a "green hard" state (i.e. before firing), were shaved or turned on a lathe, to the exact dimensions and smoothness required by the designer, although they were occasionally left with a slightly rough surface for special effects. Doulton's staff consistently won the highest awards for throwing and turning, in competitions organised by such bodies as the Society of Arts and the Worshipful Company of Turners.

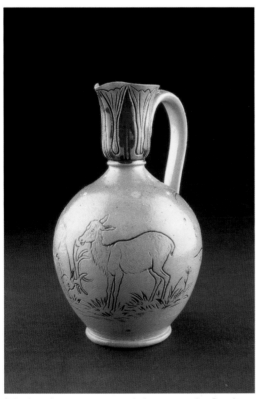

Salt-glazed stoneware jug with deer, incised or Sgrafitto technique, by Hannah Barlow, 1871-2. Doulton & Co., Lambeth. Height 21.6 cm.
Walter C. Cook Decorative Art Collection, Museum of New Zealand Te Papa Tongarewa.

Salt-glazed stoneware vase, the design of donkeys and children incised through white slip, by Hannah Barlow assisted by Lucy Barlow, 1883. Doulton & Co., Lambeth. Height 30.4 cm.
Collection: Museum of Applied Arts and Sciences, Sydney, Australia.

Decorative Techniques in Lambeth Stoneware, 1867–1914

The Lambeth artists soon developed innovative ideas and technical skills, while the Art Director, Wilton Rix, pioneered many new glazes and materials. The initial form of decoration, instigated by Tinworth but perhaps best-known through the works of Hannah Barlow, was christened *Sgraffito*. In the accepted sense, this term referred to decoration scratched or incised through a coating of white or coloured slip (semi-liquid clay) into the underlying clay body, when the pot was fresh from the wheel and the clay wet.

With most of the early Doulton Wares, however, the scratched decoration was made directly into the uncoated clay. The raised burr thus created prevented any applied colouring from spreading outside or into the pattern. In many cases the main decoration, contained within a broad band, was left uncoloured. Great accuracy and skill was demanded of the artists in incising their designs as mistakes were not easy to correct.

If the clay was left to harden for 24 hours, a deeper, scooped-out incision could be made, and the burred edge would break off. Colour added to the pattern was likewise prevented from spreading, and darker tones were achieved by cross-hatching in appropriate areas.

Patterns, often of intricate and interlocking geometric shapes, or stylized foliage, were also created by carving away the clay, creating striking tonal effects which were further enhanced by applied colours.

Left: Salt-glazed stoneware jug with frieze of hares, by Hannah Barlow, assisted by Emily E. Stormer and Annie Neal, 1876. Doulton & Co.,Lambeth. Height 22.1 cm. *Canterbury Museum Collection.*
Right: Salt-glazed stoneware flagon by Arthur Barlow, c. 1871-2. Doulton & Co., Lambeth. Height 20 cm. The leaf design and subtle colours of this flagon are characteristic of the work of Arthur Barlow. Arthur suffered ill-health and died in 1879 at the age of 34.
Hawke's Bay Cultural Trust, Hawke's Bay Museum Collection, Napier.

Left: Doulton Ware miniature biscuit barrel, with an engraved E.P.N.S. lid and handle, by Edith Lupton assisted by Alice Robjeant, 1881. Doulton & Co., Lambeth. Height 13 cm. *Private Collection.*
Right: Doulton Ware jardinière by Elizabeth Atkins assisted by Kate J. Castle, Emma A. Burrows and three unidentified helpers, 1882. Doulton & Co., Lambeth. Height 24.5 cm. The stylized foliage is carved and coloured, with a stippled ground and applied beading. This piece was originally attached to a pedestal and is typical of such wares made for conservatories and drawing rooms. *Private Collection.*

Moulds and stamps were used to produce dots, discs, medallions, and floral sprigs, which were frequently applied, along with beading. (This work would usually be done by probationers or junior assistants.)

More painterly effects were obtained (after much experimentation) by adapting the technique of *pâte-sur-pâte* decoration to stoneware. This delicate form of decoration, in which a number of coats of clear or (more usually with stoneware) pigmented slip were applied by brush or pencil to build up the design, had been introduced into England by Marc Solon. This famous ceramic artist had come from Sèvres in 1870 to work at the Minton factory in Stoke-on-Trent, producing exquisite examples on translucent bone china. Working with Rix at Lambeth, the first exponents of the new method were Eliza Banks, Florence Barlow and Eliza Simmance, who in time attained great mastery over the difficult technique. Birds formed a favourite subject matter in this style for Florence Barlow, and earned her the nickname "Birdy" Barlow. (She and Hannah had an equal facility in the depiction of animals and birds, but early on decided to divide the subject matter between them.)

John Sparkes, who retained a close association with the Lambeth Studios, commented:

Salt-glazed stoneware vase with stippled ground and *pâte-sur-pâte* bird and grasses, by Florence Barlow (assistants' marks obscured), 1883. Doulton & Co., Lambeth. Height 36.9 cm.
Collection: Museum of Applied Arts and Sciences, Sydney, Australia.

To paint with the earthy pigment requires great decision of hand and accuracy ... There are eighteen colours and tints which can now be used ... The difficulties here overcome were great and numerous, but a very accurate adjustment of flux and pigment has been worked out, so that the opaque portions burn away and become semi-transparent, showing the ground through. One great trouble was to obtain adhesion between the body and the

Left: Doulton Ware candlestick with incised decoration and high relief modelling by Mary Ann Thomson, 1880. Doulton & Co., Lambeth. Height 22.5 cm. The 1870s and 1880s saw a fashion for the grotesque – the wearing of stuffed humming birds on ladies' hats, and jewellery resembling snakes and lizards. Contemporary Japanese modelled ceramics with realistic flora and fauna reinforced this influence on a number of the Doulton Lambeth artists.
Collection: Museum of Applied arts and Sciences, Sydney, Australia.

Right: Doulton Ware vase with full-relief modelling and incised decoration. Doulton & Co., Lambeth, 1882. Height 46.7 cm.

Clearly influenced by the late 19th century Japanese pottery which was being acquired by European and British museums in the 1870s, this vase is not signed. It has been attributed to W. (A.?) Cund, a modeller about whom very little is known and who appears to have left Doulton's by 1882. It could easily, however, be the work of Hannah Barlow or even George Tinworth.
Collection: Museum of Applied Arts and Sciences, Sydney, Australia.

Doulton Ware jardinière with incised, carved, and applied beading decoration, and moulded elephant supports. The artist was George Tinworth with possible assistance from William Hollowell, 1876-80. Doulton & Co., Lambeth. Height 19.7 cm.
Private Collection.

colour; this, however, is now successfully overcome. This [technique] is absolutely new in the [stoneware] potter's art, and is a true example of the *pâte-sur-pâte* principle, inasmuch as it is not enamel but body that is the basis of the decorating material. (Eyles, 1975.)

In addition to more conventional forms for decoration were a number of original and slightly bizarre modelled wares. Principal artists involved were John Broad, Cund, Mary Ann Thomson and George Tinworth. The wares ranged from brown bear candlesticks to ashtrays in the shape of a man's head surrounded by a life-belt.

It is possible that the Doulton artists were inspired or influenced by contemporary Japanese wares – masterpieces of high-relief, elaborate modelling – which were acquired in the late 1870s by the South Kensington (now Victoria and Albert) Museum. The works attributed to Cund certainly appear to have been influenced by this source. In the early 20th century a number of these small "bibelots" were designed for reproduction by Harry Simeon, Vera Huggins and Leslie Harradine. They usually had a practical application as ashtrays and small trinket or pin trays.

Often several techniques would be combined, with the result that one item might have up to half a dozen decorators working on it. Over the years, the artists developed a number of styles and decorative fashions. Some, such as Tinworth, and Hannah and Florence Barlow, found their particular mode of expression and virtually never deviated from it throughout their long careers. Several were more receptive to external influences and artistic trends, and experimented with changing styles and techniques. Included in this category are Arthur Pearce,

Salt-glazed stoneware jug with tube-tooled outlines, stippled ground and *pâte-sur-pâte* birds, by Florence Barlow with two unidentified assistants, 1891-1901. Doulton & Co., Lambeth. Height 24 cm. *Private Collection.*

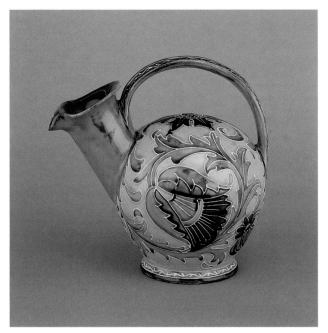

Doulton Ware water jug with carved stylized poppies and foliage by Arthur Pearce, assisted by Jane Hurst 1882-91. Doulton & Co., Lambeth. Height 21.5 cm. This unusual jug was probably influenced by contemporary interest in Persian art. *Art Gallery of New South Wales.*

Left: Doulton Ware vase, pulled and carved at the rim, with applied beading and *pâte-sur-pâte* decoration by Frank Butler, 1891-1901. Doulton & Co., Lambeth. Height 20.5 cm. *Private Collection.*
Centre: Doulton Ware vase with a typical lizard or sea serpent-like creature modelled by Mark V. Marshall, 1902-12. Royal Doulton, Lambeth. Height 27.6 cm. *Collection: Museum of Applied Arts and Sciences, Sydney, Australia.*
Right: Salt-glazed stoneware dragon on a grotto modelled by Mark V. Marshall, 1902-12. Royal Doulton, Lambeth. Height 27.3 cm. *Collection: Museum of Applied Arts and Sciences, Sydney, Australia.*

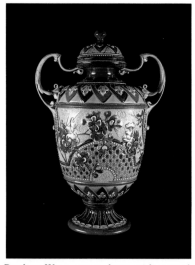

Doulton Ware covered urn with carved and incised coloured decoration, stippled ground, and *pâte-sur-pâte* blossom. Made as an Art Union of London prize, the artist was Eliza Simmance, assisted by Emily J. Partington and Louisa Russell, 1891-3. Doulton & Co., Lambeth. Height 29.2 cm. *Walter C. Cook Decorative Art Collection, Museum of New Zealand Te Papa Tongarewa.*

Frank Butler (a deaf and almost dumb artist, described by Sparkes in 1874 as "... one of many thus heavily afflicted who have passed through the [Lambeth Art] school."), Harry Barnard and Eliza Simmance – who, perhaps to go with her modern image, preferred in her later years to be known as Elise. Others – as in the case of Mark V. Marshall – apparently sought to escape the confines of traditional forms and fashions altogether.

A feature of the Doulton Lambeth Studios was that all the decorators were allowed to sign their work. Often this meant that the base of a pot was covered with a profusion of marks, from the stamped initials or letters identifying the junior assistants to the incised monogram of a major artist. Tinworth was the only artist who was normally permitted to put his mark on the actual body of the work. Some examples of Hannah Barlow's work have been found signed in this manner, but it is likely that these were exhibition or specially-commissioned pieces. As most of the marks were recorded in the illuminated address of 1881, it is possible to identify the people responsible for many of the wares found today.

During the 1870s and 1880s, dates were added to the company trademark – until retailers complained that this made it difficult to sell old stock.

Other Developments at Lambeth, 1872-1914

It was not long after establishing the Doulton Wares, that Henry Doulton gave the go-ahead to Rix and Sparkes to explore further methods of promoting art pottery. Over a period of some 40 years, from about 1872, a host of "Wares" appeared from the Lambeth Studios. They incorporated a number of new or re-developed glazes and a variety of bodies.

The first was *Lambeth Faience*, a product which met with much public success. This had only a superficial likeness to the tin-glazed products of 17th century Europe (also known as maiolica or delftware). Whereas the European Faience decoration was painted on an opaque unfired lead glaze containing tin oxide, Lambeth Faience was decorated on a once-fired (biscuit) body, and subjected to glazing and further firings. W. P. Rix formulated a suitable warm-coloured earthenware body. After the first firing, designs were painted on in vitrifiable colours made from metallic oxides and applied in an oil medium. A special department was established to train the Faience artists. They were required to have a confident and steady hand in applying the pigments to the still-porous biscuit bodies, and the imagination and artistic abilities to cope with the often quite radical changes which the colours underwent in the kiln.

Lambeth Faience plaque, portrait of a girl in a mob cap, by Katherine Sturgeon, 1881. Doulton & Co., Lambeth. Diameter 43.2 cm. The style of dress of the subject appears to have been influenced by the "Aesthetic" movement.
Collection: Museum of Applied Arts and Sciences, Sydney, Australia.

Left: Lambeth Faience vase with tulips by Mary Butterton, 1874-77. Doulton & Co., Lambeth. Height 18.2 cm. This piece is painted on an earthenware blank manufactured by Pinder, Bourne & Co., of Burslem, a firm taken over by Doulton & Co., in 1877. Earthenware bodies for Faience were made at Lambeth by about 1879. *Collection: Museum of Applied Arts and Sciences, Sydney, Australia.*
Right: Lambeth Faience vase with Sturt's Desert Pea flowers, by Katherine B. Smallfield, 1891-1902. Doulton & Co., Lambeth. Height 20 cm. Designs for a number of pieces featuring Australian wildflowers were sent to Lambeth during the 1890s by a Miss Rutherford of Bathurst, New South Wales. *Collection: Museum of Applied Arts and Sciences, Sydney, Australia.*

Lambeth Faience plaque by James Cruikshank, 1878. Doulton & Co., Lambeth. Diameter 52 cm. The portrait of a man in a broad-brimmed hat with a steel gorget, and border of urns, shields, foliage and mythical creatures is in the style of 16th century Italian maiolica wares.
Collection: Museum of Applied Arts and Sciences, Sydney, Australia.

After a second firing, to fix the colours, the piece was dipped in glaze, and re-fired in a muffle kiln, which protected the wares from direct contact with the fire. At first a lead glaze was used, producing warm, yellowish-brown tones; this was replaced with a colder, whitish-toned leadless glaze after 1900. Any further decoration of the wares – overglaze enamelling, modelling, *cloisonné* or gilding – required yet another firing. Many items – vases, tazzas, plaques, tiles – were produced in Lambeth Faience, the designs being flowers and foliage, portraits, landscapes and various types of stylized ornamentation.

While the colours were generally harmonious, the standard of painting amongst the exponents of Faience Ware was not consistently high. However, the leading artists – among them John Eyre, James Cruickshank, and later Margaret E. Thompson (a talented artist who specialised in scenes from fairy tales, nursery rhymes and children's stories) – often produced masterly works in the genre.

Impasto Ware was claimed as an original Doulton invention. (It is necessary to treat with some caution any such statements – Doulton's advertising department was no less adept than its rivals in ignoring

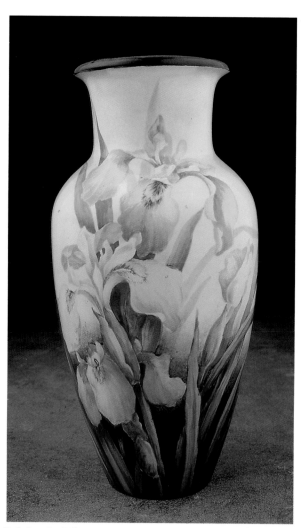

Left: Lambeth Faience vase with irises, unknown artist, 1891-1914. Height 27.5 cm. *Private Collection.*
Right: Lambeth Faience vase, with fairy and white butterflies, by Margaret Thompson assisted by Minnie Webb, 1891-1901. Height 26 cm. *Art Gallery of New South Wales Collection.*

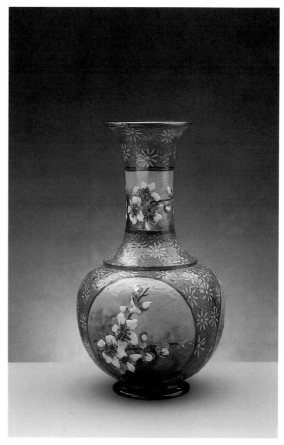

Left: Impasto vase with crocuses, unknown artist, 1879. Doulton & Co., Lambeth. Height 26 cm. *Private Collection.*
Right: Impasto vase with blossoms and daisies, by Fannie J. Allen 1883. Doulton & Co., Lambeth. Height 36.6 cm. *Collection: Museum of Applied Arts and Sciences, Sydney, Australia.*

the efforts of others.) Utilizing an earthenware body similar to that employed in Faience Ware, the artist applied coloured pigments in a fairly thick slip to the raw clay. As described by John Sparkes, co-originator with Rix, this:

> ... models the form as well as paints it. The small amount of relief that is thus given to the ornament ... adds to the apparent reality of the thing depicted. Impasto painting, therefore, has all the advantages that opaque tempera or oil painting possesses, inasmuch as it reflects light from its surface.

Made mostly between 1879 and 1906, Impasto Ware was not particularly durable and is much rarer than either the salt-glazed Doulton Wares or Lambeth Faience.

Silicon Ware and *Chiné Ware* are among the more commonly found examples of Doulton Lambeth products. Silicon Ware is distinguished by its body – smooth, extremely hard stoneware, fired at very high temperatures, either with or without a salt-glaze. The former has no gloss, while the latter has a very faint, eggshell gloss or "smear". It was produced in a natural terra-cotta colour, or in a variety of self-colours – greens, browns, black, bronze, grey and off-white – through the introduction before firing of coloured stains. Introduced in 1880 and

Silicon Ware vase with perforated, incised, and *pâte-sur-pâte* decoration, by Edith Lupton assisted by Rosetta Hazeldine, 1882. Doulton & Co., Lambeth. Height 40.9 cm. *Collection: Museum of Applied Arts and Sciences, Sydney, Australia.*

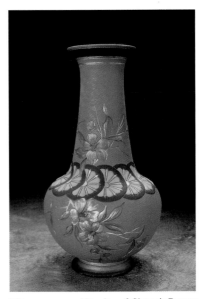

Silicon ware and Doulton & Slater's Patent vase with floral decoration, by Eliza Simmance assisted by Louisa Russell, 1885. Doulton & Co., Lambeth. Height 26 cm. *Walter C. Cook Decorative Art Collection, Museum of New Zealand Te Papa Tongarewa.*

in steady production until 1914, Silicon Ware was decorated in a variety of ways, similar to those employed on the salt-glazed stonewares. In addition, much use was made of applied coloured clays, blue and white on buff or pale brown being especially fashionable.

Chiné and *Chiné-Gilt Wares* refer to particular types of decoration, either with or without gilding, usually on a stoneware body. The process was jointly patented by Doulton and John Slater (manager of the Burslem factory) and went into production in 1885. It involved pressing lace, net or other textured fabrics into the wet clay to obtain a relief pattern. This acted as a background to further decoration using the usual techniques either on-glaze or under-glaze, or sometimes the two combined. Production of these labour-intensive wares continued unabated until 1915, and spasmodically from 1919 to 1939.

Natural Foliage Ware was related to Chiné Ware, in the sense that it employed the same technique of impressing objects into the wet clay, and decorating the resultant pattern. Introduced originally as *Repousée Ware* in 1883, it featured a range of salt-glazed stoneware vases, garden and flower pots. Real leaves were pressed into the clay, removed, and the impression painted in naturalistic colours – soft red-browns, greens and blues. Once glazed, the effect was very realistic – at first sight it appears as if actual leaves have been sealed in under the glaze. Such was its popularity, that this ware – renamed Natural Foliage – continued in production until the 1950s, although on a much diminished scale after 1914. The range was extended to include teapots, beakers, mugs, pin-trays and other items.

Left: Natural Foliage Ware vase with impression of fern leaves. Assistants' marks for: (?) Fanny Sayers, (?) Miss H. Toland, Elizabeth Shelley, Edith H. Woodington, 1891-2. Doulton & Co., Lambeth. Height 28 cm. *Private Collection.*
Right: Natural Foliage Ware teapot with concentric bands of leaves, by Senior Assistant Maud Bowden, post-1902. Doulton & Co., Lambeth. Height 13.2 cm. *Collection: Museum of Applied Arts and Sciences, Sydney, Australia.*

Terracotta Wares had been made at Lambeth since the 1820s, with garden statuary being introduced by Henry Doulton in 1840. White terra-cotta garden urns and decorative columns were exhibited by Doulton & Watts in the Great Exhibition of 1851 in London. Later Lambeth designers of terracotta sculptures included John Broad and Arthur Pearce, but pre-eminent in the field was George Tinworth.

Of particular interest are his religious panels with which he had numerous exhibition successes. Tinworth received many important commissions for public buildings such as York Minster Cathedral (the reredos), the Guards' Chapel, and the English Church of St Alban in Copenhagen. He calculated that by 1894 he had produced at least 500 of "important size", and innumerable smaller ones. The scenes were drawn from both Old and New Testament stories, of which Tinworth had a profound knowledge, and often displayed evidence of his quirky sense of humour. The larger religious panels had to be cut into sections when soft and reassembled after firing, on a reinforced concrete base.

The base colour of Tinworth's panels is a pinkish-brown, and sometimes has a white wash to highlight certain figures or features. The bulk of these works was done prior to 1902, although Tinworth continued to work in his Lambeth studio until his death in 1913.

In contrast to the previous wares, there was a number of ceramic developments at Lambeth which were never produced in great quantities, either because of their limited appeal or because of the cost of production.

Terracotta garden statue, the woman with flowers probably representing *Flora*. The designer is unknown, but possibly John Broad, 1890s. Royal Doulton, Lambeth, 1902-23. Height 130 cm. *Private Collection.*

Terracotta panel by George Tinworth, c. 1905, *Rebekah Leaving Her Father's House To Get Married. Gen. 24,58 A Time To Get And A Time To Lose.* Length 53 cm; height 28.5 cm. *Canterbury Museum Collection.*

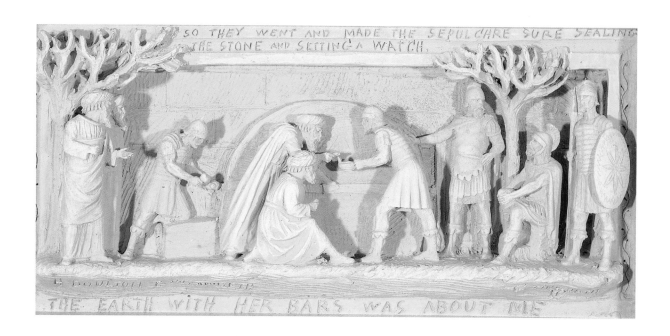

34

Some objects which appear from time to time seem to have been purely experimental, "one-off" pieces. *Simulated Wares* were curiosities produced sporadically from the late 1880s to 1914. One such was Black Leather Ware which used a very dark matt Silicon stoneware body, into which real leather was often impressed to obtain a more realistic effect. A popular shape was the "black-jack" or jug, in which even the stitched seams were imitated. Other wares imitated copper (complete with riveting, dents and verdigris), iron and other metals. Various lustre glazes were used to achieve a metallic sheen, and electroplating seems also to have been employed, both here and at Burslem.

Marqueterie Ware (a term borrowed from cabinet-making, where it referred to a method of wood inlay decoration) was "invented" in 1886 by Wilton Rix. It was patented the following year under the names of Doulton & Rix. Because of the high production costs, due to its method of manufacture, it was not a viable commercial concern, and was withdrawn in about 1906.

It was related to 17th century agate or onyx ware, in which the characteristic patterning was not just surface decoration but an integral part of the object. The clays used were either naturally coloured or were stained, chiefly in tones of blue, brown and white. Chunks of clay were sliced thinly, then interleaved to form the desired patterning. The entire mass was then compressed into a solid block about 10-12 centimetres square. This process could be repeated any number of times. The patterned clay was then modelled or press-

Opposite:
Top: Terracotta panel by George Tinworth, c. 1882, *So They Went And Made The Sepulchre Sure Sealing The Stone And Setting A Watch. The Earth With Her Bars Was About Me.* Length 36 cm; height 18 cm. At least one other copy of this work exists. It varies slightly in detail due to Tinworth's practice of working over the piece before it was fired.
Hawke's Bay Cultural Trust, Hawke's Bay Museum Collection, Napier.
Centre: Terracotta panel by George Tinworth, c. 1882, *And They Were Exceeding Sorrowful And Began Every One Of Them To Say Unto Him, Lord is it i. There Were Great Searchings Of Heart.* Length 36.5 cm; height 18.5 cm.
Hawke's Bay Cultural Trust, Hawke's Bay Museum Collection, Napier.
Bottom: Terracotta panel by George Tinworth c. 1877-84, *Hamam Taking Mordecai Through The Streets Of Persia. Let Him That Thinketh He Standeth Take Heed Lest He Fall. A Lesson For Prime Ministers.* Length 61.5 cm; height 28 cm.
Hawke's Bay Cultural Trust, Hawke's Bay Museum Collection, Napier.

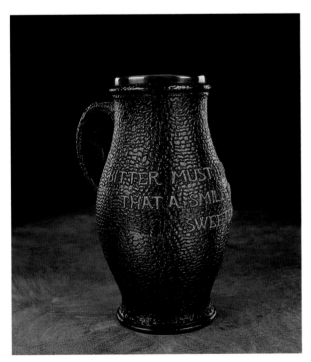

Left: Leather Ware jug (Silicon Ware body) with a silver rim, *Bitter must be the Cup that a Smile will not Sweeten,* 1889-90. Doulton & Co., Lambeth. Height 17 cm. The intention of the unknown designer of this piece was to imitate a "black jack" of the mid-17th century. *Private Collection.*

Right: Electroplated earthenware jardinière with a "brass" finish. The six scenes from Classical mythology include *Vulcan's Forge, Orpheus and Pan* and *Icarus.* It is unsigned and bears only an impressed stamp DOULTON'S. Height 30 cm. *Private Collection.*

Left: Marqueterie Ware cornucopia vase, unknown designer. Doulton, Lambeth, 1891-1906. Height 16.9 cm.
Collection: Museum of Applied Arts and Sciences, Sydney, Australia.
Right: Cararra Ware vase with daisies, designer unknown, signed by assistant Miss K. Heywood and two others. Doulton & Co., Lambeth, 1891-1901. Height 33 cm. *Private Collection.*

Velluma Ware candlestick with "print-and-tint" landscape. Royal Doulton, Lambeth, 1911-14. Height 22 cm. *Private Collection.*

moulded to the desired shape. While gilding was used to highlight the pieces, the chief interest of this ware was in its mosaic or marbled effects.

The resulting articles, many by Mark Marshall who delighted in such complexities of design, are extremely light and delicate – to find one undamaged is extremely rare. A major problem which had to be overcome in the production of Marqueterie Ware was the differing shrinkage rates of the various clays when fired.

Carrara Ware was another type of stoneware, with a white matt glaze which resembled Italian Carrara marble – hence the name. The decoration was usually done with coloured pigments. It was made mainly from 1887 until about 1903 when production dwindled.

Velluma Ware is a rare Lambeth product – it was manufactured only between 1911 and 1914. Transfers from etchings by Pearce and Rowe were printed on glazed earthenware shapes supplied by Doulton's Burslem factory. These prints, usually landscape or figures, were lightly tinted by hand. During the final firing, at about 1000° Centigrade, the colours sank into the whitish, parchment-like glaze, giving a singular effect to the finished ware.

Final Years at Lambeth

The Doulton Lambeth wares had reached the peak of their fame and production by the turn of the century. Doulton's had not been the first commercial ceramic firm to establish an "Art Pottery Studio", but the comparative success of the Lambeth enterprise had far-reaching effects. Throughout the United Kingdom potteries of all sizes started art departments, in acknowledgement of a philosophy which successfully promoted the harmonious marriage of art and industry. The products of this philosophy considerably enhanced the international prestige of British ceramics, and in many ways the activities at Lambeth foreshadowed the movement which led to the development of modern studio pottery.

Henry Doulton had been knighted in 1887, the first potter to be so honoured. In 1901, the new King, Edward VII, presented the company with his Royal Warrant of Appointment, and bestowed the privilege of using the word *ROYAL* to describe Doulton products.

By the end of the next decade, however, changing fashions in home decoration saw a distinct tailing off in orders for the highly-decorated wares which looked increasingly old-fashioned in the less-cluttered and simpler Edwardian house. In addition, the innovative ceramics introduced since the late 1870s were running at a loss. Unlike the Burslem factory there was no compensating production of other sorts of wares when demand for the purely ornamental slowed or ceased, and as staff members died, retired, or left to get married, they were not replaced. From 370 in 1897, their number decreased to 120 in 1909, 90 by 1914, and in 1925 was down to 25.

Slip-cast vase, abstract Art Nouveau pattern designed for mass production by Harry Rowe. Royal Doulton, Lambeth, 1910-22. Height 14.8 cm. *Walter C. Cook Decorative Art Collection, Museum of New Zealand Te Papa Tongarewa.*

All the pots decorated by the leading artists continued to be unique pieces, and the same high standards of quality control were retained by Joseph Mott, the Art Director who succeeded Rix in 1897. Younger artists such as Harry Simeon, Margaret Thompson and William Rowe designed and executed simpler shapes and decoration, more in keeping with contemporary trends, particularly Art Nouveau.

Most of the Lambeth wares other than salt-glazed stonewares were discontinued in 1914 with the outbreak of the Great War, when many of the male throwers, turners, glazers and others volunteered or were called up for army service. The market for luxury art wares virtually disappeared overnight, and the factory concentrated on practical items – acid-resisting chemical stoneware for explosive devices.

After the War it proved increasingly difficult to recruit new apprentices in London. By this time virtually all the potteries, except for Doulton and a few small businesses, had ceased production. Industrial pollution – added to by the muck pouring out of the coal-fired kilns – had reached such levels that there was considerable agitation to close down the remaining potbanks.

In the 1920s there was a revival of an earlier Persian Style (which had been confined in the 1880-90s to tiles). Vases, bowls and plaques were added to the range, designed mainly by Rowe, but with some by Simeon. They utilized the techniques of construction and decoration

Left: Vase, Art Nouveau design of leaves, clouds and birds, by an unknown artist. Royal Doulton, Lambeth, 1902-22. height 18 cm. *Hawke's Bay Cultural Trust, Hawke's Bay Museum Collection, Napier.*
Right: Persian Ware vase with Iznik-style foliage motifs, designed for mass production by Harry Simeon and William Rowe. Royal Doulton, Lambeth, 1922-36. Height 15.5 cm. *Private Collection.*

found in Near Eastern Iznik wares – a coarse biscuit body, coated with white slip which was painted, then re-glazed and re-fired. By 1936 production of these works, which was on a limited scale, had ceased altogether.

During the 1920s and 1930s an entirely different style of stoneware was produced under Mott's direction. In many ways it paralleled contemporary developments in the early studio pottery movement, typified by potters such as Bernard Leach. Mott preferred simple, functional shapes and decoration and was strongly influenced by Chinese traditions. Like Noke and Bailey at Burslem, Mott constantly experimented with new bodies and glazes. Artist designers such as Vera Huggins produced many pieces which excited considerable attention when shown at the Royal Academy, and at exhibitions throughout the world.

During the Second World War, much of what was left of the Art Studios was again given over to production related to the war effort. Only a very small number of stoneware pieces were produced – mainly by Vera Huggins – for export. Home market production resumed in 1950, but on a very limited scale. Agnete Hoy, a Danish-trained potter who had worked with Natalie Krebs, and later for Bullers of Staffordshire, was invited to assume control of the Art Studio.

Hoy was inspired not only by the early Lambeth artists and their salt-glazed stoneware techniques, but also by ceramists working in traditions as diverse as 17th and 18th century Europe and contemporary African cultures. She developed a new type of decoration – flowers, foliage, birds and so on painted under-glaze on a fine stoneware body with natural cream colouring. As with the earlier artists she was permitted to sign her work – initials on the pieces designed for limited reproduction, and her full name on the unique items.

These works were the harvest of an Indian summer. Costs, changing social conditions – not least of which was the passing of the *Clean Air Act* – and a transformed urban landscape had made inevitable the closure of the Lambeth Pottery. In 1956 a unique alliance between art and industry came to an end.

The story of Royal Doulton decorative ceramics did not of course finish at this point – a chapter continues to this day, but it is necessary to go back some 79 years to pick up the narrative.

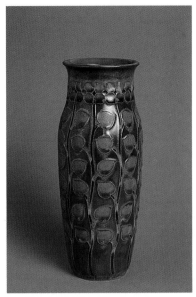

Salt-glazed stoneware vase with stylized foliage by Harry Simeon. Royal Doulton, Lambeth, 1922-27. Height 23 cm. *Hawke's Bay Cultural Trust, Hawke's Bay Museum Collection, Napier.*

Burslem – The "Bung Hole Without a Barrel"

Hispano-Moresque earthenware wall plaque, with a design by John Slater featuring a mermaid, lobsters and birds. Doulton & Co., Burslem, 1891-1901. Diameter 31 cm. *Collection: Museum of Applied Arts and Sciences, Sydney, Australia.*

*I*n 1877 Henry Doulton had purchased an interest in Pinder, Bourne & Company of Burslem, Stoke-on-Trent – right in the heart of the traditional home of the English ceramic industry, North Staffordshire. Despite the reputation which his industrial products and the more recent art pottery had won, Doulton's venture was regarded with scepticism, and a degree of scorn by the rather complacent Staffordshire potting "establishment".

The Nile Street potbank was a medium-sized concern – 160 workers and eight bottle-ovens – producing a typical mid-Victorian array of middling quality earthenwares for domestic use. The owner, Thomas Shadford Pinder, had long desired to lift his firm's products out of this mediocrity and into the dizzy realms of "higher ceramics" (as he termed it) populated by such firms as Wedgwood, Minton, Spode, Derby and Worcester. Lacking the necessary flair and cash, he eventually approached Henry Doulton. The latter was interested in extending his reach into the area of fine earthenware, and saw the proposition as a challenge.

The partnership was a disaster and the lack of progress both frustrating and financially unacceptable. (Some of the Lambeth staff disparagingly referred to the money-draining venture as a "... bung hole without a barrel".) In 1880, a general reorganization of the works and the staff took place, and in 1882 Pinder accepted a retiring settlement. The firm became Doulton & Co., Burslem.

The young decorating manager, John Slater, an accomplished and recognised ceramic artist, was appointed as Art Director. Henry Doulton further astonished the interested onlookers by appointing an even younger man than Slater – 23 year old John Cuthbert Bailey – as General Works Manager. Slater and Bailey were an ideal team. For some years the more successful of the Pinder, Bourne patterns continued to be reproduced, but Bailey weeded out a multitudinous variety of unprofitable decorative wares. Slater did an enormous amount of research into different ceramic bodies, grounds, and reduction glazes. For example, he revived the traditional *Hispano-Moresque Ware* – lustre-painting on tin-glazed earthenware which is fired in a reducing atmosphere – enhancing the ancient technique with original iridescent effects.

In addition Slater developed a number of new styles of decoration. In *Spanish Ware*, flowers, foliage and scroll-work were outlined with delicately-traced gold, in combination with on-glaze painting and raised paste, on a vellum or ivory ground. Some of the vases and ewers in this style have elaborate dragon handles or even moulded dragons crawling across the surface. This opulent ware was very popular during the 1890s and early 1900s.

Spanish Ware: Cabinet plate with briar roses by Walter Slater, 1886-91 (diameter 23 cm); vase (with handles) decorated with Australian wild flowers by Louis Bilton, 1888-91 (height 37 cm); faceted vase with poppies, unsigned, 1886-91 (height 26.5 cm). Doulton & Co., Lambeth. *Canterbury Museum Collection* (plate); *Private Collection.*

Chiné Ware, a Slater invention, has been described under the Lambeth wares, but it was in fact produced at both factories.

Another invention of Slater's, patented in 1889, was a photographic process for transferring designs to pottery. This was a very useful alternative method to engraving for delicate lines, which were then gone over with gilt traceries, or filled with paint. It was also commonly used in the reproduction of photographs for transfer to souvenir or commemorative wares, and to rack plates.

Bone China at Burslem

Both Burslem and Lambeth artists worked with Slater in producing the new designs but it became increasingly obvious that the fine earthenware imposed limitations on what could be achieved. Pressure was put on Henry Doulton to build a new factory for the production of bone china, the English equivalent of porcelain, which had been invented in the 18th century. However, the decorated earthenware was barely paying its way, and Henry was not at first convinced.

His capitulation, in 1883, was sudden and not without drama. Slater had received a valuable order from the United States for a new set of tableware designs by Fred Hancock, but only on condition that the

Bone china vase on plinth, hand-painted by Harry Tittensor, 1902-22. Royal Doulton, Burslem. Height 110 cm.

Tittensor drew his inspiration from a variety of sources and was capable of working in many contrasting styles. *Museum of New Zealand Te Papa Tongarewa.*

work be executed on bone china. He decided to send some samples, painted on a batch of glazed white porcelain which he had especially acquired from Limoges. If they were approved, Slater intended to use them in one further attempt to convince Doulton to produce bone china.

Unhappily, Henry Doulton sighted some of these samples before matters were explained to him. In an uncharacteristic rage he smashed virtually the lot, sweeping them to the factory floor with his umbrella. Slater and Bailey were immediately suspended, and the unfortunate traveller who had brought the order was sacked on the spot.

To everyone's surprise, Doulton reappeared the next morning, and instead of closing down the factory, as not a few anticipated, he reinstated the staff and calmly announced his intention to build a china works. Having slept on the matter, he had realised the superiority of Hancock's work on a porcelain body. If Doulton of Burslem was indeed to rival Wedgwood, Minton and the others, the standard of ceramic bodies had to equal the decorative abilities of his staff.

From 1884, the factory was expanded successively. Fine earthenware was used for good tableware and less expensive ornaments. Bone china was reserved for expensive tablewares, elaborate tea and dessert services, fish and game plates, and hand-painted, highly decorated vases and other ornaments.

One of Slater's first tasks had been to build up a team of gifted artists, designers, modellers and gilders. This group was to be encouraged (in Henry Doulton's words) to "... forget ... most of what was done here in the past." Slater's original band was increased with the expansion into bone china wares. It is significant, and a contrast to the Lambeth Studios, that, in keeping with the Staffordshire tradition, these artists were all men – almost to this day women in the "potteries" have usually been confined to the uncreative and repetitive tasks.

Hand-painted ewer vase (and detail), depicting Australian waratahs, by Louis Bilton, c. 1892. Doulton & Co., Burslem. Height 68 cm. It is possible that this is one of the vases painted for the World's Columbian Exposition at Chicago in 1892-93. It was probably designed by John Slater. The modelled figures and ornate gilding patterns suggest the work of Charles Noke and Robert Allen. *Collection: Museum of Applied Arts and Sciences, Sydney, Australia.*

Left: Hand-painted bone china covered vase, *Venus and Amorini*, by Charles Labarre, c. 1892. Doulton & Co., Burslem. Height 42.5 cm. Labarre of Paris was engaged by Slater in about 1891 to work at Burslem for a year on some of the special vases intended for the World's Columbian Exposition at Chicago in 1892-93. Labarre was especially recognised for his paintings of Cupids and classical figures in the Sèvres style. This vase was originally part of Cuthbert Bailey's personal collection, and was sold by John Bates in the late 1920s. *Private Collection.*
Right: Hand-painted bone china vase, *The Knight Errant*, by Harry Tittensor. Royal Doulton, Burslem, 1902-22. Height 44 cm. *Private Collection.*

In addition to Robert Allen, William Hodkinson, Walter Slater (John's nephew), Samuel Wilson and others, numerous artists were "head-hunted" from rival potteries – Edward Raby and Fred Sutton from Worcester; David Dewsberry from Hill Pottery; John Hugh Plant and Harry Piper from Coalport; Joseph Birbeck, Henry Mitchell and Louis Bilton from Minton; Edwin Wood and John (Jack) Hewitt from Wedgwood; George Buttle from Moore Brothers; Thomas Phillips and Charles Noke from Worcester.

Within a few years, younger, equally gifted artists were being trained at the Nile Street factory, in association with local Schools of Art at Burslem and Hanley, and further afield – South Kensington and Lambeth. These included many names which were also to make Doulton Burslem famous – George White, Harry Allen, Percy Curnock, Arthur Eaton, Walter Nunn, Harry Fenton, Charles Beresford Hopkins, Leslie Johnson, Harry Nixon, Jack Price and Harry Tittensor.

Left: Hand-painted bone china vase with continuous scene of women, girls and cats in drawing room, by George Buttle, 1905. Royal Doulton, Burslem. Height 70 cm. This vase was exhibited at the New Zealand Exhibition of Art and Industry, Christchurch, in 1906. *Private Collection.* **Right:** Hand-painted bone china vase on revolving base, with a continuous scene of a boy and cattle in a rural landscape, by Charles Beresford Hopkins, 1902-17. Royal Doulton, Burslem. Height 69 cm. Hopkins' work was very popular with the Australian and New Zealand market. *Private Collection*

From the 1890s onwards the Doulton Burslem artists, drawing inspiration from the Classical, Renaissance, Baroque, Roccoco, Oriental, and many other styles, including those of the Pre-Raphaelites, Symbolists and Impressionists, began to create a school of their own. Slowly a distinctive "Doulton" quality began to emerge, as it had previously at Lambeth. Charles J. Noke was an outstanding example of these men who had been encouraged and inspired by "the freedom and the promise" which (in his own words) working for Henry Doulton offered. He later succeeded Slater as Art Director, and was to become one of the most influential figures in the extraordinary success of the Burslem wares, confirming Doulton's instinct that while "... to distinguish between eccentricity and genius may be difficult ... it is surely better to bear with singularity than to crush originality".

Extremely fine earthenware bowl with hand-painted feather decoration by Joseph Birbeck Snr. Royal Doulton, Burslem, 1902-22. Height 5.2 cm; diameter 10.5 cm. *Private Collection.*

Harmonies of Colour

*T*he period 1890-1940 saw the outpouring of an incredible range of decorative art products from the Burslem works. The hand-painted wares which are such a feature of New Zealand, Australian and North American collections are high quality pieces which represent the upper end of the broad market for which Doulton catered.

A new style of ceramic painting, particularly with floral subjects, was developed. By 1913 it was being emulated in all the other leading ceramic factories. W. Turner, in the March 1913 volume of *The Connoisseur,* wrote:

> Pottery painters at all the classic factories worship the god "stipple". The brush with the finest point was the only one used for finish. In this style, however, the richness, the breadth, the atmosphere and the colour are all obtained with the broad flat wash. The colours are all transparent and can only be obtained by continued re-firing one thin glaze over the other.

William Owen, in *The Royal Doulton Artists* (1910), considered that "... a Doulton vase with its flower-woven beauty and its harmonies of colour, shows the art of the potter in its highest expression."

Edward Raby was the pre-eminent artist in this field. Sketching straight from nature, his oils and water-colours took on new depths

Left: Bone china vase, hand-painted sprays of sweet peas by Edward Raby, 1902-19. Royal Doulton, Burslem. Height 49.5 cm *Art Gallery of New South Wales Collection*
Right: Bone china covered urn-vase, with hand-painted sprays of pink and cream roses by Edward Raby, 1912. Royal Doulton, Burslem. Height 31.8 cm. *Collection: Museum of Applied Arts and Sciences, Sydney, Australia.*

Left: Bone china covered vase with hand-painted sprays of roses, by Edward Raby, 1902-5. Royal Doulton, Burslem. Height 79.5 cm. *Canterbury Museum Collection.*
Right: Bone china covered vase with hand-painted sprays of roses, by Edward Raby, 1902-5. Royal Doulton, Burslem. Height 66 cm. *Private Collection.*

These vases were both exhibited by John Bates at the N.Z.I.E., Christchurch, 1906, and are illustrated in the photograph from his pavilion.

Bone china vases, hand-painted by Edward Raby: (tall) *Fair in My Garden Buds the Rose*, 1902-19, height 50.7 cm; and (pair) landscapes painted in the Cadbury Gardens, England, 1913, height 18 cm. Royal Doulton, Burslem. *Private Collections.*

of expression and colour (especially in the reds) when translated onto the ceramic canvas.

J. F. Blacker, ceramic expert and critic for *The Connoisseur Magazine*, described:

> Mr E. Raby at work in his studio painting roses with a full brush upon a large vase ... As a painter of roses he has no superior. What struck me was the wonderful grace in the grouping of the flowers all around the vase, the masterly quality of broad expression, free from niggling and stippling, and the general softness and richness of the colouring. But I understood these, when his book of studies lay open before me. In them were the records of the roses; blooms growing in the open air, studies of groups and single flowers from the greenhouse. These lovely flowers become glorious on porcelain, immortalised by the artist, who, seeing their souls, took them into his own.

David Dewsberry was described by Blacker as:

> ... a veteran flower painter, the master of the Orchid, for in depicting this glorious exotic he has no equal...a dessert set by Dewsberry is considered "the thing" nowadays.

Dewsberry had the run of the conservatories of many famous orchid-growers of the day – the Duke of Sutherland and Mr Joseph Chamberlain among others. William Owen commented, "His close observation enables him to paint this flower with striking fidelity to the delicacy of its varied tints, the boldness of its rich colouring; the quality of the true artist is further displayed in the agreeable grouping of these aristocrats of Flora's kingdom." (The orchid could be considered the quintessential

Left: Bone china urn, hand-painted orchid decoration by David Dewsberry, 1902-12. Royal Doulton, Burslem. Height 45 cm. This is believed to have been the centrepiece in the Burslem showroom during the visit by King George V and Queen Mary in 1913. *Private Collection.*
Right: Bone china urn with hand-painted orchids by David Dewsberry, 1902-20. Royal Doulton, Burslem. Height 32.5 cm. *Private Collection.*

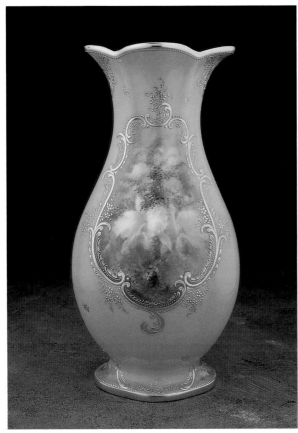 

One of a pair of bone china vases (and reverse view) with orchid decoration by David Dewsberry, c. 1913. Royal Doulton, Burslem. Height 31.5 cm. *Private Collection.*

Edwardian flower; no entrance hall, dining table, boudoir, or garland for a ball-gown was considered complete without it.)

Percy Curnock, apprenticed in 1885 at age 13 and with Doulton's for over 69 years, was another exponent of roses. He was also renowned for his beautiful depictions of many other flowers, from gardens or hedgerow. William Owen saw Curnock as an artist "... who possesses the quality of thoroughness ... conscientious execution and attrac-

Left: Bone china covered urn with gilded filigree foliage and hand-painted spray of Chelsea-style flowers by Percy Curnock, 1902-22. Royal Doulton, Burslem. Height 15 cm.
Collection: Museum of Applied Arts and Sciences, Sydney, Australia.
Right: Bone china biscuit barrel with silver cover and handle, and hand-painted blue and white roses by Percy Curnock, 1891-1902. Doulton & Co., Burslem. Height 15 cm. *Private Collection.*

47

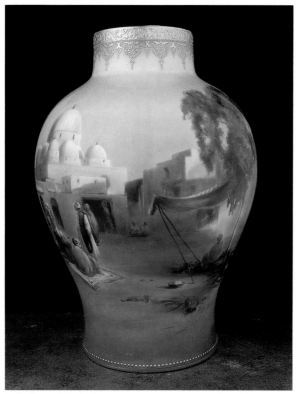

Left: Bone china vase with continuous scene, *Bab Souika – Arab Tunis,* by Harry Allen, 1911. Royal Doulton, Burslem. Height 42.5 cm. *Private Collection.*

Right: Bone china vase with hand-painted continuous scene of the Tunisian town, *Kairouan,* by Harry Allen, c. 1911-22. Royal Doulton, Burslem. Height 29.5 cm. *Private Collection.*

Bone china dish with hand-painted scene and four reserves of young missel thrushes by Harry Allen 1914. Royal Doulton, Burslem. Length 27.5 cm; width 21.5 cm. *Private Collection.*

Bone china dish, *The Gulf of Venice,* hand-painted by John Hugh Plant, 1915. Royal Doulton, Burslem. Length 26.5 cm; width 20 cm. *Canterbury Museum Collection*

tive style". Over the years he also produced many fine landscapes, and designed material for lithographed tableware patterns.

Harry Allen, son of Art Department Head, Robert Allen, was one of Doulton's most versatile artists, and was equally famous for his Middle Eastern scenes, his flowers and birds. He was one of the earliest Royal Doulton figurine painters, and from 1924 this occupied him fully.

Leslie Johnson painted many vases, comports, dessert services and so on in the style of Fragonard, Watteau and Wheatley. He decorated the panels for later versions of the *Dante* vase, including the one shown at the Christchurch Exhibition of 1906 and now in the possession of the Museum of Applied Arts and Sciences, Sydney. Johnson was also called upon, on occasion, to reproduce the original work of other Doulton artists. In the late 1920s an important New Zealand collector ordered, through John Bates, a magnificent revolving vase with hand-painted scenes by George White (whose career with Doulton had finished in 1912). The vase was duly sent from the factory in Burslem, but on arrival was found to have been badly cracked in transit. A study of the damaged original enabled Johnson to make an exact copy, finished in 1930, for the sum of £40 – the original had cost £120. Doulton's also repaired the original and the collector finished up with both versions.

Left: Bone china vase with two panels in the style of an 18th century landscape with figures, hand-painted by Leslie Johnson, 1902-5, and exhibited by John Bates at the Christchurch Exhibition in 1906. Royal Doulton, Burslem. Height 71 cm.

This is one of several later versions of the *Dante* vase exhibited at the Chicago World's Columbian Exposition in 1892-93. The original was modelled by Charles Noke, the gilding and decoration designed by Robert Allen, with painted scenes by George White and Charles Labarre. The figures on the base of the plinth represent Dante and Beatrice, supported by Fame and Poetry. Those on the handles are Knowledge and Power, in the forms of an aged man and an autocrat. The seated figure on the lid is Jupiter.
Collection: Museum of Applied Arts and Sciences, Sydney, Australia.

Centre: Bone china vase on a revolving base, with scenes of a woman, children and amorini, hand-painted by Leslie Johnson after George White, 1930. Royal Doulton, Burslem. Height 65.7 cm. *Private Collection.*

Right: Bone china vase, *The Bathers*, hand-painted by George White, 1902-05. Royal Doulton, Burslem. Height 29.3 cm. This was one of the ten George White pieces exhibited by John Bates at the N.Z.I.E., Christchurch, 1906, which were awarded a gold medal.
Canterbury Museum Collection.

John Hugh Plant's particular talent, lay in landscape painting, and he appears to have been especially fond of Venetian scenes "… of age-mellowed beauty, with the rosy glow or perfect blue of soft Italian skies".

George White, who had trained at the Lambeth and South Kensington Art Schools, rapidly became Burslem's chief painter of figural subjects. William Owen considered that White's work took:

> … a prominent place in any exhibit of Doulton ware. It is beautiful and correct in form, delicate and attractive in its expression of the character and colour of his subjects. In portraiture White attains the happy success of not only "catching" the likeness of his subject but in seizing and expressing personality – the supreme test of the portrait painter.

Examples of White's "likenesses" include portraits of Sir Henry Doulton, and the eldest daughter of John Bates of Christchurch. Many of White's works seem to have been inspired by the school of late 19th century British academic painters who delighted in allegorical themes, with the subjects depicted in pseudo-Classical draperies.

Bone china plaque of a woman teaching a young child the violin, hand-painted by George White, 1902-12. Royal Doulton, Burslem. Height 25 cm; width 20.4 cm (framed). *Private Collection.*

Left: Bone china wall plate, *Ophelia*, with peacock and floral border, hand-painted by George White, 1903. Royal Doulton, Burslem. Diameter 22.5 cm. *Private Collection.*

Right: Bone china wall plate, *Ellen Terry as Portia in the Guise of a Doctor of Laws*, hand-painted by George White, 1909. The three reserves within the border of gilt scrolls and classical "masks" contain scenes from the *Merchant of Venice*, described on the reverse: [1] *The Trial Scene. Shylock claims payment of his bond;* [2] *The Casket Scene. Bassanio's choice;* [3] *The Flight of Jessica and Lorenzo. My daughter! O my ducats!* Royal Doulton, Burslem. Diameter 26 cm. *Private Collection.*

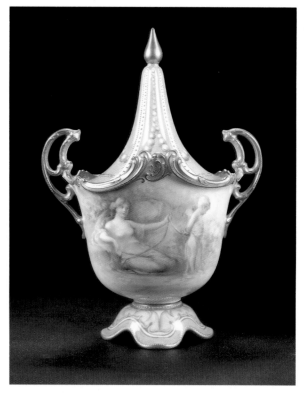

Left: Bone china Sèvres-style covered vase, *Captive Cupid*, Venus holding Cupid with ribbons, hand-painted by George White, 1904. Royal Doulton, Burslem. Height 23.3 cm. *Private Collection.*

Right: Bone china vase, *Love's Pilotage*, with Venus and Cupid in a shell boat, hand-painted by George White, 1886-91. Doulton & Co., Burslem. Height 18.6 cm. *Collection: Museum of Applied Arts and Sciences, Sydney, Australia.*

New Paths

S later's early developmental work with decorative techniques, glazes and ceramic bodies, was continued in association with Noke, and the artists themselves. The new decorative styles, incorporated with fine bone china and parian-style bodies, included Hyperion, Luscian, Lactolian, *Pâte-sur-Pâte* and Lustre wares, and most rarely enamelled pieces which are quite distinct from the usual on-glaze enamel painting on china. Noke was chiefly responsible for this turn-of-the-century technique, which involved relief modelling combined with luminous transparent enamels, built up in successive layers, and re-fired at least three, and up to six times. The procedures were related to champlevé and *cloisonné* in metal enamelling. Some pieces were extensively gilded, the gold being applied in the final firing. The enamelling technique was applied to panels, plaques, tiles and large flat dishes, but because it was both risky and expensive, it is thought that probably no more than about a hundred were ever made. The examples which survive commonly depict Classical themes, such as *Juno, Vanity's Bird*, or were inspired by poetry – *Isabella and the Pot of Basil*, shown at the 1906 New Zealand Exhibition, is derived from a

Enamelled panel, *Isabella and the Pot of Basil*, by Charles Noke and William Hodkinson, 1891-1900. Doulton & Co., Burslem. Height 31.7 cm; width 23.2 cm.

This panel was one of the three exhibited at the 1906 Christchurch Exhibition by John Bates & Co., which were awarded a gold medal. The title comes from the poem by John Keats. *Private Collection.*

Enamelled panel, *Dolce Far Niente*, by Charles Noke and William Hodkinson, 1891-1901. Doulton & Co., Burslem. Height 18.4 cm; width 18.5 cm.
Art Gallery of New South Wales Collection.

Over page
Top: Enamelled panel, *Vanity, Juno's Bird*, by Charles Noke and William Hodkinson, 1891-98. Doulton & Co., Burslem. Height 17.8 cm; width 29.5 cm.

This piece was purchased from Doulton & Co. for £21 in 1899.
Art Gallery of New South Wales Collection.
Centre: Enamelled panel depicting a woman with an amorino, Charles Noke and William Hodkinson, 1898. Doulton & Co., Burslem. Height 8.7 cm; width 19.3 cm.
Art Gallery of New South Wales Collection.
Bottom: Panel with ceramic frame and enamelled depiction of the god Pan, with two women, by Charles Noke and William Hodkinson, 1891-1901. Doulton & Co., Burslem. Height 21.5 cm; width 39.5 cm.
Collection: Museum of Applied Arts and Sciences, Sydney, Australia.

52

work by John Keats, Noke's favourite poet. Noke seems to have often worked with William Hodkinson, an exceptionally skilled gilder and designer, on these jewel-like miniatures.

The *Hyperion* style of painting, entirely hand-executed, is distinguished by its very delicate manner and colours, and the "modern" style in which the (mainly) floral subjects were depicted. It was sometimes combined with *pâte-sur-pâte* decoration. The name was suggested by Keat's *Dream of Hyperion*.

Luscian was described in the *Pottery Gazette* of May 1898, as achieving "... a rich, soft effect by the skilful blending of various colours painted on the glaze". The glazing and firing methods caused the colours to sink into the glaze producing an unusual, almost underglaze, effect. Pieces occasionally bear a special backstamp with the word Luscian. Subject matter for these pieces is often the country landscape or flowers. More rarely figural themes can be found. Artists who worked with this technique include Edward Raby, Fred Hancock and Walter Nunn.

A parian-type body invented by Slater in the early 1890s was adapted for use in a particular type of *pâte-sur-pâte* decoration christened *Lactolian*. The name presumably derives from the Latin for milk, and would refer to the milky consistency of the diluted clay or slip (white or coloured) which was painted on in layers, to build up a

Bone china Lactolian Ware vase with sea horses and Art Nouveau-style flowers, 1902-22. Royal Doulton, Burslem. Height 15.8 cm.
Collection: Museum of Applied Arts and Sciences, Sydney, Australia.

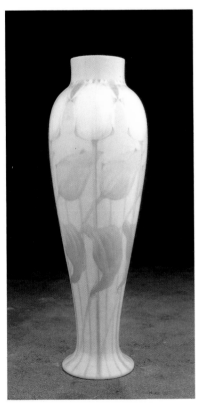

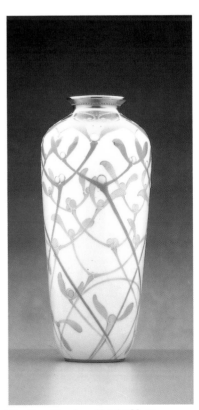

Left: Bone china Hyperion Ware vase with tulips in the Art Nouveau style, 1902-22. Royal Doulton, Burslem. Height 33 cm. *Private Collection.*
Centre: Bone china Luscian Ware vase, *God Bless Her*, hand-painted by Walter Nunn for Queen Victoria's Diamond Jubilee in 1897. Doulton & Co., Burslem. Height 28 cm. *Private Collection.*
Right: Bone china Lactolian Ware vase with mistletoe and gilding, by Walter Slater and Richard Ridgway (gilder), 1902-1905. Royal Doulton, Burslem. Height 28 cm. *Collection: Museum of Applied Arts and Sciences, Sydney, Australia.*

Bone china vase with *pâte-sur-pâte* poppies, outlined with gilt, by Walter Slater, 1886-1891. The modelled mount at the foot has a vellum glaze. Doulton & Co., Burslem. Height 24.5 cm.
Collection: Museum of Applied Arts and Sciences, Sydney, Australia.

bas-relief decoration on the unfired clay shape. The process was slow, as the slip had to be left to dry between coats. Finally the relief forms were smoothed, incised and modelled to the artist's satisfaction, and coated with a final thicker slip. Gilding was often added and the piece was then glazed and fired. A single, medium size vase could take a month to complete, and even in 1900 cost £100-£200, limiting its market to a few connoisseurs. It remained in production for only a few years.

A less complex method of *pâte-sur-pâte* or raised decoration – similar to that used on the Lambeth stonewares – was used on bone china vases and other ornaments, often combined with on-glaze painting and gilding. Thomas Phillips and Walter Slater were two of the artists who produced work in this medium.

Lustre Wares were produced either by painting over a special glaze with pigments containing metallic particles – gold, silver, platinum and copper, or in some cases including them within the glaze itself. During the second firing in a reducing atmosphere (that is, one in which the oxygen content was lowered), the particles formed a thin, shimmering film on the surface. In some later examples lustre effects were combined with Flambé and Titanian glazes.

From the mid-1890s Charles Noke gradually turned his attention from modelling to the development of new glazes and different types of wares. Among the first of these developments was a ware which he named *Holbein*. This utilized one of Slater's hard-fired porcelain bodies with a special transparent ivory glaze. Decoration often combined low-relief modelling and/or coloured clay inlays, with the motifs inspired by 'old masters' portraits. Other pieces had entirely original art work – portraits, or scrolls and stylized foliage. J. M. O'Fallon, writing in the *Art Journal* of February 1896, described the appearance of the glazed and fired Holbein Wares as having "... a

Left: Holbein Ware jardinière, tavern scene with a Royalist tippler and two Puritans, by Walter Nunn, 1902-10. Royal Doulton, Burslem. Height 34 cm. *Private Collection.*
Right: Rembrandt Ware jardinière, portrait of an old judge with the motto, *Corruption Wins Not More Than Honesty*, by Harry Tittensor, c. 1902-15. Royal Doulton, Burslem. Height 28 cm. *Private Collection*

Rembrandt Wares: copper-covered vase with, *Self Portrait*, after Rembrandt and the motto, *A Contented Mind Is A Blessing Kind,* by Arthur Eaton, 1898-1901. Doulton & Co., Burslem. Height 38 cm; cylindrical vase, *King Charles I* (after Van Dyck), by Walter Nunn, 1902-10. Royal Doulton, Burslem. Height 42.6 cm.
Collection: Museum of Applied Arts and Sciences, Sydney, Australia.

decidedly Rembrandtish chiaroscuro in parts ... [keeping] the imagination busy at play through its endless lights and shades of burnt sienna, the prevailing colour". Production continued, although not on a large scale, until about 1915. Sometimes a special backstamp identifies the ware, but this was not always used.

A similar style of decoration was used in the *Rembrandt Wares*, produced from about 1898 to 1915. The body, however, is quite different, being a robust, Staffordshire unrefined marl (a clay containing carbonate of lime), similar to that used in the saggars or fireproof containers in which pottery was fired to protect it from the heat of the kilns. Some of the larger Rembrandt pieces were supplied with copper or pewter stands and covers – several of these are recorded as having been executed by the inmates of the Duchess of Sutherland's Cripple Guild. Coloured slips stained with metallic oxides were used for the paintings, which were then richly glazed. A typical feature of this ware is the portraits, based on works not only by Rembrandt, but also by Van Dyck, Holbein, Velasquez, Frans Hals and others. Curiously, the decorative scrolls and friezes and the lettering of the characteristic 'mottos' are very much in the Art Nouveau style. Apart from Noke, the

Rembrandt Ware vase, windmills in a winter landscape and motto, *Doth My Simple Feature Yet Content You,* by Walter Nunn, 1902-10. Royal Doulton, Burslem. Height 33 cm.
Canterbury Museum Collection.

artists chiefly responsible for this ware were Arthur Eaton, Walter Nunn and Harry Tittensor.

Landscapes and seascapes were also painted in coloured slips – usually in a rather impressionistic style – as were trees, foliage, flowers and birds. These were generally much lighter in colouring, but employed the same marl body as Rembrandt Ware.

Kingsware was another form of slip-decoration, produced in great quantities between about 1898 and 1946, and considered very collectable today. Unlike the other decorative wares discussed, Kingswares were slip-moulded. Coloured slips – soft greens, yellows and russets – were poured into the parts of the mould with the impressed figure or other design work; the mould was then fully assembled and the dark brown slip generally used for the body was added, whereupon the different slips adhered to one another without mixing. After a period of time the surplus slip was poured off, the mould left to dry and the shape eventually removed. A transparent ivory glaze was fired over the different coloured slips producing a singular and pleasing finish. The subject matter and shapes found in Kingsware are equally varied. The most collectable shapes have been the whisky flagons which were used for advertising by firms like Dewars. A special line of flasks with silver fittings was produced as prestige products to be sold by retailers – these did not have brand names. There are over 70 different subjects found on the Kingswares, ranging from Dickens characters to Bonnie Prince Charlie.

Queensware (introduced about 1932) is similar to Kingsware in production method, shapes and decoration, but has an ivory body. Similar to both Kingsware and Queensware is *Embossed Ware* (1935-39). The same moulds, colours, forms and methods of production were used as in both the above, but the subjects were painted after the first firing. Brown colour was airbrushed onto handles, spouts and inside the neck.

Collection of Kingsware, Queensware and Embossed Ware: *Hooked, Micawber, Here's a Health unto His Majesty, Nelson, Uncle Sam, Pied Piper.* *Private Collection.*

56

Bold Manipulations

*P*erhaps the most exciting and "potterly" developments which occurred in the late 19th and early 20th century at Burslem, were the experiments with transmutation glazes. They took place at a time when European potters were beginning to appreciate the inherent appeal of glazes as a sole means of decoration.

Rouge Flambé

For many years, European (particularly French) porcelain manufacturers had sought to reproduce a glazing technique, perfected by the early Chinese ceramists, which yielded an exquisite ruby red (Sang de Boeuf), and mottled or streaked glazes (Rouge Flambé, Peach Blow, and Haricot). Originally, all that was known about these "chemical curios" was that some form of copper oxide produced the rich red colours after the porcelain was fired in a reducing atmosphere. When the supply of air to the kiln was limited, carbon monoxide was produced; this took up or reduced whatever oxygen was exposed to it. The copper oxide was reduced to cuprous oxide, and produced a lustrous rich red colouring. Adding more oxygen to the atmosphere (oxidizing), produced shades of green, which could be extended into sky blues by still further oxidization. Albert Jacquemart described the process of this transmutation glazing:

> Now, these combinations may be effected in the furnace by means of bold manipulation...Placed at a given moment in these various conditions, the "Haricot" glaze assumes a most picturesque appearance, the whole surface of the vase becomes draped with faint and streaky colorizations, changing and capricious as the flame of spirits.

Gold Flambé double gourd vase, 1904-6. Royal Doulton, Burslem. Height 13.5 cm. *Art Gallery of New South Wales Collection.*

Slater, Noke and J. C. Bailey determined that Doulton Burslem would not be left behind in the efforts to master the processes which were required to place production on a viable commercial footing. (Joseph Mott at the Lambeth works was also involved in experimenting with transmutation glazing, but on stoneware bodies.) Publicity pamphlets written for Royal Doulton in the early 1900s, contemporary exhibition reports, and later books on Doulton wares, have tended to overstate the role played by the firm in the "rediscovery" of these glazes. Chemists working at Sèvres in the late 1840s had met with some success, as had other French and Austrian companies. The famous ceramic chemist Hermann Augustus Seger (inventor of the cones for measuring kiln temperatures), who worked for the Royal Berlin factory between 1878 and 1890, claimed to have been the first European to put Sang de Boeuf glazes into commercial production in the 1880s.

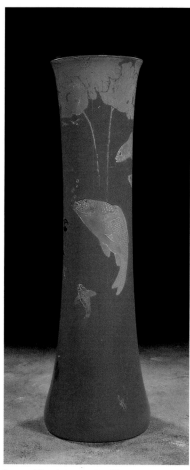

Rouge Flambé vase, by Charles Noke and Cuthbert Bailey, with gilded carp and water lilies by William Hodkinson, 1904-5. Royal Doulton, Burslem. Height 52 cm.

This was one of the gold medal pieces exhibited at the New Zealand International Exhibition of Art and Industry, Christchurch, 1906, by John Bates & Co.
Private Collection.

A number of these porcelains were exhibited at the World's Columbian Exhibition in Chicago in 1892-3, where they would almost certainly have been seen by representatives from Doulton – it was at this exhibition that the first major display of Burslem Art Wares was staged. All of these developments were equally familiar to Bernard Moore, who was among the first of the English potters to have some success, although on a small scale, with flambé, crystalline and other transmutation glazes.

By 1900 the Doulton team had, like the Europeans, produced some good specimens but at great cost. At this point they were joined by J. C. Bailey's son, Cuthbert Bailey, an astute young chemist. His scientific training, enthusiasm and physical endurance made him ideally suited to the long and arduous experiments which went on for the next three years. These involved not only theoretical and practical research work and analysis, but the physical building, re-building and firing of special kilns. He worked with Charles Noke, who had developed a particular interest in this field where his extensive knowledge of colours and glazes was invaluable, and with Bernard Moore. As a result of his successes in transmutation glazing, Moore had been engaged as a consultant in 1902. By 1904 Bailey, Noke and Moore had firmly established the conditions under which the glazes could be reproduced with certainty, and the Doulton wares were officially launched into the world at the St Louis Exhibition in the United States.

A report in *The Journal of Commerce,* 16 August 1904, on the "… 'Rouge Flambé' Pottery at St.Louis …" effused that the Doulton team had "… penetrated the secret of the ancient potters of China, and achieved that success which has so captivated visitors at St.Louis and the art connoisseurs of Europe." C. F. Binns, writing in the *American Ceramic Society Transactions,* Vol.VII, Part 1, 1905, was less captivated:

Two novelties must be noticed. The copper red of Doulton and the coloured glaze work of the Ruskin pottery by Mr W. Howson Taylor. In the former case it is evident that too much has been claimed. A special pamphlet blazons forth the rediscovery of a lost art … The colors are indescribably rich, but the ware is not a rediscovery of Chinese copper red, nor has the art of this production ever been lost.

The *Art Journal* for April 1905, while acknowledging that this criticism had some merit, pointed out that the Doulton Flambés could certainly "… vie with the best examples of the East" and futhermore had the additional merit of "… that element of control which is the best guarantee of progress". It was never possible, however, with these or any of the subsequently-developed transmutation glazes, to totally predict the results of the chemical reactions which occurred in the kiln, and so no two pieces were ever exactly alike.

The "progress" predicted by the *Art Journal* is strikingly evident in the pieces which were sent to New Zealand for the 1906-7 Exhibition. Included were mottled flambé vases of various shapes, and others with golden carp and finely delineated water lilies, or dragons in turquoise enamel relief, on luminous flambé grounds.

Left: Flambé vase with an enamelled and gilded Chinese dragon, by Charles Noke and Cuthbert Bailey, 1904-5. Royal Doulton, Burslem. Height 22.5 cm. This was one of the gold medal pieces exhibited at the New Zealand International Exhibition of Art and Industry, Christchurch, 1906, by John Bates & Co. *Canterbury Museum Collection.*
Right: Flambé vase with a gilded eagle by Harry Nixon, c.1910-20s. Royal Doulton, Burslem. Height 20 cm.
Hawke's Bay Cultural Trust, Hawke's Bay Museum Collection, Napier

Left: Flambé vase with a stencilled design of mermaids and fish, 1920s. Royal Doulton, Burslem. Height 18.4 cm.
Canterbury Museum Collection.
Right: Flambé pomegranate vase, signed by Noke and Fred Moore, c. 1945-50s. Royal Doulton, Burslem. Height 17.3 cm.
Hawke's Bay Cultural Trust, Hawke's Bay Museum Collection, Napier.

Left: "Landscape" Flambé vase with an under-glaze print of a country cottage and garden, c. 1910-20s. Royal Doulton, Burslem. Height 27.5 cm. *Private Collection.*
Right: Flambé jardinière with enamelled and gilded Viking ship, c. 1904-20. Royal Doulton, Burslem. Height 42 cm.
    A very similar design and decorative technique is found among wares produced by Bernard Moore after he set up his pottery in 1905. This illustration was also used later by Noke for one of his Series Wares. The original price for this piece was £38/10/-.
Private Collection.

Pair of Flambé embracing apes, c. 1910. Royal Doulton, Burslem. Height 13 cm. *Private Collection.*

Cuthbert Bailey resigned in 1907, and Bernard Moore had already left – in 1905 – to open up his own factory for the production of specialist art wares. Charles Noke was given the major responsibility for the further development of transmutation glazes. Under his direction, later experiments produced flocculated blue and violet markings, feathered and veined effects, and the incorporation of engraved or painted landscapes whose dark tones merged with the lustrous red glaze.

On the whole, production of these wares dwindled from the early 1930s, with changing tastes and rising production costs. The last true experiments with the flambé glaze were in the early 1950s. A black flambé – advertised as Rouge et noir – was introduced in 1953, but so great was the expense that it was withdrawn after only six months. Some of the animal figurines which had been brought out in the early 1900s are still in production today, while other, more contemporary sculptures (including figures) have recently been added.

Crystalline Wares

Bailey and Noke, perhaps at the instigation of Bernard Moore, had become interested in controlling what is technically a defect in the glazing and firing process. Characteristic groupings of radiating or elongated crystals of various sizes and shapes form in glazes containing zinc oxides, if the wares are cooled too slowly during a certain stage of the firing process. The Sèvres factory had pioneered a technique of deliberately inducing and controlling this phenomenon in the 1880s, and it was also developed by artist potter Clément Massier near Cannes, Royal Copenhagen in Denmark, and Meissen in Germany.

The Doulton potters formulated a special porcelain body which could take the required glaze at a steady temperature of 1400° Centigrade for some hours. Output was limited because they had to be fired separately from any other products, and even the slightest variation in temperature would ruin the desired effects. By 1918, production, always on a fairly limited scale, had ceased.

Crystalline Wares were shown at the 1906-7 Christchurch Exhibition, both by John Bates and by the firm itself in the Official British Government Arts and Crafts Exhibit. Together with the flambé products, they met with great acclaim. Here, as at later exhibitions in Brussels, Turin and Ghent, collectors and appreciative ceramic experts soon purchased virtually every piece. Ivory and all-white pots predominated, but Noke took great delight in experimenting with coloured glazes such as a rich blue, turquoise, yellow, red and brown.

Crystalline Wares by Charles Noke (left to right): yellow glaze, c. 1904-18 (height 16.9 cm); blue glaze vase, beaten metal lid with ceramic button, 1904-5 (diameter 11 cm); onion vase with white glaze, 1904-5 (height 27.8 cm). Royal Doulton, Burslem.

The blue and white vases were shown by Royal Doulton in the British Government Exhibit, Arts and Crafts Section, at the New Zealand International Exhibition of Art and Industry, Christchurch, 1906. *Otago Museum, Dunedin* (Yellow); *Private Collection.*

Titanian vase, *Out in the Cold, Pierrot Disconsolate*, by Harry Tittensor, 1915-25. Royal Doulton, Burslem. Height 23.2 cm. The original price for this vase was £10-10-6. *Mrs Noeline Bain.*

Titanian Wares

Introduced in 1915, *Titanian Ware* was hailed with rapture and unabashed patriotism by J. F. Blacker. In his booklet, *Fairyland on China*, Blacker firmly stated the case for Titanian Ware:

> [It] is immensely superior to any modern products of China or Japan; but more than that, it is English, and eminently suited to any scheme for the decoration of the Homes of England ... There is great variety, and each [form] is clothed with its delectable glaze, a coat of soft, throbbing colour – greenish-grey, merging into tender blue, or graduating through shades of grey into the most mellow tints of greens and blues ... Picture the direct antithesis to those bad forms and glaring colours which you see with amazement in the homes of your friends. Well! most of them were made in Germany or Austria, and the money paid for them has formed part of the enemies' war chest. "Yes!" I hear you say, "never again!" ... Here are vases painted with exquisite flowers ... birds and animals in their natural habitats:- here, gulls skimming above the waves, or bullfinches perching upon the branches of a tree; there, a polar bear in the Arctic region surrounded by snow and ice, or rabbits peering through a haze; and amongst them I noticed a peacock in full plumage perched upon a tree – a remarkable piece of painting ... When the people patronise porcelain production, success comes to that manufacturer who strives continually to satisfy his clientéle ... The plain duty of the people of our Empire – it should be esteemed a privilege – is to buy British porcelain; it is the best.

Jingoism aside, Blacker's florid prose gives a good description of these somewhat ethereal wares, which had (and have) considerable

Left: Titanian vase, white cat on a branch, with blossom spray, by Harry Allen, c. 1915-23. Royal Doulton, Burslem. Height 17 cm. *Private Collection.*
Right: Titanian bowl, polar bear and cub on ice floes, by Harry Allen, c. 1915-23. Royal Doulton, Burslem. Diameter 15.8 cm. *Canterbury Museum Collection.*

Pair of Titanian vases by Harry Tittensor, 1918, with scenes from *The Rubaiyat of Omar Khayyam.* Royal Doulton, Burslem. Height 44 cm.
Left: The inscription on the base is Quatrain 37:
Ah fill the cup: What boots it to repeat,
How the time is slipping underneath our feet,
Unborn tomorrow and dead yesterday,
Why fret about them if today be sweet.
Right: Only the title remains, *The Potter's Shop* (Quatrain 36).
Private Collection ; Dunedin Public Art Gallery Collection .

public appeal. A large quantity certainly seems to have found its way to the farthest reaches of the Empire, probably through Shorter and Bates, and is found today in the private and public collections of Australasia.

Another Noke development, and the result of three to four years experimentation, the Titanian glazes (which contained a compound of the metallic element titanium) were fired on a specially-developed body akin to Chinese egg-shell porcelain – translucent but particularly strong. The artists especially associated with Titanian Ware were Robert and Harry Allen, F. Henri, Harry Tittensor, Percy Curnock and Harry Nixon. Edward Raby also painted some of the early pieces (he retired in 1919), and it is possible that his peacock vase in this ware is the example referred to in Blacker's article. Titanian was also utilised in tea and coffee services, items of tableware and rack plates. Although some items were made to special order in the early 1930s, production had largely ceased by 1925.

Titanian vase, hand-painted peacock on a branch with blossoms, by Edward Raby, 1915-19. Royal Doulton, Burslem. Height 34.5 cm. *Private Collection.*

Sung Glaze Ware

Sung vase with fish and seaweed, signed by Noke and Fred Allen, c. 1928-40. Royal Doulton, Burslem. Height 13.5 cm. *Hawke's Bay Cultural Trust, Hawke's Bay Museum Collection, Napier.*

During the Great War (1914-18) the normal luxury trade was greatly reduced, and Noke, with more time to spare, concentrated his efforts on special bodies and glazes. In so doing he created a new family of transmutation glazes, which he christened *Sung*, as a tribute to the old Chinese master potters. Although the name was not used on the wares until 1919-20, many pieces marked with a *FLAMBÉ* backstamp clearly fall into the Sung category.

Often using double reductions and double oxidization, the wares were characterised by a greatly-extended range of colours and subtle tonings, often combined with lustre effects. Sometimes the glaze was superimposed over another type of glaze such as Titanian, and many had underglaze painting or printing with exotic birds, dragons, animals, flowers such as prunus blossom, and foliage. Splashes of white and turquoise enamel and delicate gold traceries were also added, as with some of the early Flambé pieces.

Noke worked in association with Harry Nixon. Underglaze painted Sung was produced in quantity until about 1940, and according to an interview in 1983, with post-war Sung artist, Fred Moore, continued in production on a reduced scale until the early 1950s.

Left: Sung vase with under-glaze illustration of gnomes (unsigned), c. 1930s. Royal Doulton, Burslem. Height 28 cm.
The design on this vase was also used, with several variations, in the very popular *Gnomes* Series wares, and is reminiscent of the work of illustrator Arthur Rackham. The original price label is for £52-10-0. *Art Gallery of New South Wales Collection.*
Right: Sung vase with mottled effects, signed by Noke and Fred Moore, 1947. Royal Doulton, Burslem. Height 33 cm.
Walter C. Cook Decorative Art Collection, Museum of New Zealand Te Papa Tongarewa.

Sung pomegranate jardinière, with floral under-glaze decoration, on-glaze enamelling and gilding; signed by Noke and Harry Nixon, c. 1932-40. Royal Doulton, Burslem. Height 60.5 cm; diameter 53 cm. Formerly in the collection of John Bates & Co., New Zealand, this is reputedly the largest Sung piece ever made by Royal Doulton.
Collection: Museum of Applied Arts and Sciences, Sydney, Australia.

Sung bowl with peacock, unsigned, 1920-30s. Royal Doulton, Burslem. Diameter 37 cm. The peacock became a favourite image in the late 1860s when Japanese art reached Europe. With the sunflower, it was one of the most popular symbols of the Aesthetic Movement of the 1870s and 1880s, and was used extensively by the Doulton artists for many years.
Private Collection.

Chinese Jade

This unusual ware was also introduced in 1920, the product of some seven years of patient research by Noke, and latterly Nixon. It is possible that Noke was trying to reproduce a ceramic described as "false jade" in early T'ang literature. The results were quite remarkable – a pure white glaze with veining in greens and turquoise, which certainly justify its name. Produced in small quantities until the 1940s (and for a short period afterwards), the forms included various vases, a lamp base, two-handled goblet and powder bowl, a seated Buddha and a female Chinese figure, lily (or lotus leaf) bowls, an elephant, llama, horse, two fish and a leaping salmon.

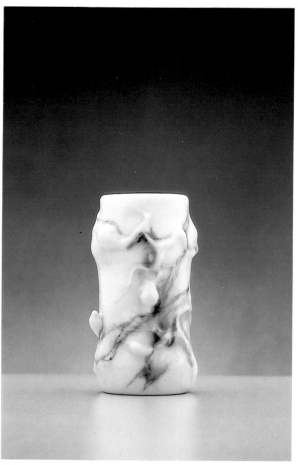

Chinese Jade vase with low-relief foliage, signed by Noke, 1930.
Royal Doulton, Burslem. Height 14.7 cm.
Collection: Museum of Applied Arts and Sciences, Sydney, Australia.

Chang Wares

Noke, Harry Nixon, and Noke's son Cecil John (known as Jack) continued research into the transmutation glazes and in 1925 announced an entirely new Ware – *Chang*. This was introduced into New Zealand by John Bates at the 1925-6 South Seas Exhibition held in Dunedin. Noke, or probably the extremely efficient publicity depart-

Left: Chang vase, signed by Noke and Harry Nixon, c. 1925-30s. Royal Doulton, Burslem. Height 32 cm. *Museum of New Zealand Te Papa Tongarewa Collection.*
Right: A collection of Chang Wares, signed by Noke and Nixon, c. 1925-30s. Royal Doulton, Burslem. (Vase) Height 17 cm; (goblet) Height 10.5 cm; (bowl) Height 4.3 cm; (bottle) Height 22 cm. *Private Collection.*

ment at Royal Doulton, was somewhat excessive in the advertising of these wares:

> Chang the Elder, one of the greatest master potters of all time, lived during the Southern Sung Dynasty (1127-1279 A.D.). He was especially famed for his crackled ware and brilliantly coloured glazes which, like those of others of the same period, European potters have sought for centuries to evoke anew, but in vain. Here again, after countless experiments, Doulton's have bridged the centuries ...

Chang the Elder probably never existed, and wares such as these had not been seen in China or elsewhere. The *Pottery Gazette* more accurately described them as "... one of the most startling ranges of new ornamental pottery that has seen the light of day for over half a century."

Difficult for the general public to accept readily (then and now), the majority of Chang Wares were nevertheless hailed as masterpieces of ceramic art by connoisseurs and collectors. In contrast to Flambé and Sung, the new wares used a much heavier earthenware body in order to withstand the characteristic layers of glutinous, iridescent and brightly-coloured glazes, which often ran in tongues of varying sizes and densities down the sides of the form. Usually the topmost layer was deliberately crackled. From about 1935 bone china bodies were used. Forms found in the Chang Wares include classic Chinese vases and bottles, dishes, snuff-bottles, lamps in the form of a potter working under a canopy, and a flower bowl with a sinuous dragon modelled by Noke. Production of Chang Ware was continued on a very limited scale after 1939, finally ceasing in the late 1940s.

Art and Utility

"Blue Children" Series ware: pilgrim flask, with gilt tracery and scenes of a woman by the seashore, by W. Brown, and a woman and child in a garden. Height 36 cm. This piece does not have a Doulton backstamp, but has a Robert Allen Studio number on one foot. *Private Collection.*

*A*s with the industrial base of the Lambeth works, at Burslem, Doulton's financial stability rested, not on the experimental wares or pieces of special aesthetic interest but on the mass production of tablewares and less expensive types of ornamental pottery. Here too the ethic of "art and utility" prevailed – good and interesting design in form and decoration, well-potted wares. Because of this the borderline between "decorative" and "functional" is hazy.

The Series Wares

The Doulton Series Wares are possibly the perfect illustration of art and utility. They provided a way of using a large number of standard blank shapes – rack or wall plates, vases, jugs, trays, tea sets, candlesticks, beakers, and even chamber pots. (They also provided work for the artistic team when trade in "art" wares was slack.) The brain-child of Charles Noke, they were originally marketed as Novelty Art Wares or Fancy Lines. They were intended to "… adorn yet serve some useful purpose …", and it was hoped they would appeal to every taste in terms of decoration and colour scheme.

From the start (about 1900) Noke had the "collector mentality" in view, and people were encouraged to acquire whole sets of various topics. The subject matter ranged from legends, songs, literature (the

Bunnykins wares: Plate, *Feeding the Baby*, by Barbara Vernon, 1943 (diameter 16.8 cm); *Be Prepared* DB56, 1986 and *Brownie Bunnykins* DB61, 1987 (both height 10.5 cm). Royal Doulton, Burslem.

Father Rabbit (in the plate) is a thinly-disguised portrait of the artist's father, Cuthbert Bailey, General Manager at Royal Doulton. *Private Collection.*

characters of Charles Dickens were a particular favourite) and history, to popular activities such as hunting, fishing and motoring. The nostalgic longing for "days of yore" was often exploited, with scenes of Olde England – of countryside, towns and people long gone. Animal and floral studies were firm favourites, and many a generation has grown up with the specially designed nursery series such as Bunnykins, Nursery Rhymes, and more recently, Brambly Hedge.

Fine earthenware or, less commonly, bone china bodies were used. All decoration was printed, but a variety of techniques was used. These included block printing and silk screening, transfer printing from engraved plates and lithography (both of which were combined with hand-colouring – the so-called "print-and-tint" method), and a specially-patented photographic process. The usual finishing utilised a pale yellow or ivory glaze, although a dark yellow (Holbein) was sometimes employed to give a particularly rich effect. Titanian glazes were also used, but a less-common effect was Celadon which emulated the famous, pale-green Chinese glaze.

Other early Burslem artists besides Noke worked on the development of the Series designs, but few besides Noke have their signatures on the actual items. Those principally involved included Walter Nunn, Arthur Eaton, Harry Tittensor and Cecil Noke. There is today indignation in certain quarters that Noke attached his signature to many of the Dickensware designs, as they were almost exact copies of illustrations by well-known late Victorian artists such as Kyd. As these were derived in turn from the characterisations of earlier artists (Cruikshank, Phiz, Leech, and others), who had illustrated the original publications, the resentment seems misplaced. So popular were the Dickens

Top: "Arabian Nights" Series Ware: Rack plate, *Ali Baba's Return*, 1909-28. Royal Doulton, Burslem. Diameter 24 cm. *Private Collection.*
Bottom: Plaque, *Harvest*, Brangwyn Ware, 1931. Royal Doulton, Burslem. Diameter 32 cm. *Private Collection.*

Dickensware Series: Shaving mug, *Sam Weller* (height 11.5 cm); sugar sifter, *Sairey Gamp* (height 16.3 cm); cheese dish (Canute), *The Fat Boy* (illus.), *Barkis*, and *Poor Jo* (height 13 cm; maximum diameter 26 cm). *Private Collection.*

stories, and such was the familiarity of the public with the outward appearance of such characters as Pecksniff, Mr Pickwick and the Fat Boy, that to present them in any other guise would have been pointless – and a commercial disaster.

In addition to the Doulton stable of artists, well-known illustrators of the day had the rights to some of their works acquired by Royal Doulton – one of the few potteries to cultivate the public taste in this area. Among those universally known are Charles Dana Gibson, David Souter, Cecil Aldin, Randolph Caldecott and H. M. Bateman.

Rack plate, *A Widow and Her Friends,* c. 1906. Royal Doulton, Burslem. Diameter 26 cm. Doulton acquired the rights to use designs from the books of Charles Dana Gibson, popular American satirist and illustrator. *Private Collection.*

Production of Series Wares was interrupted by World War Two (although a number of patterns had already been withdrawn in the 1930s). Following the War the concept declined still further in popularity, and by the 1960s little more than rack plates with photographic scenes, flora and fauna, were being produced. More recently, the production of decorative plates has been revived, with themes such as Valentine's Day and Christmas. They are sought primarily by plate collectors and are not the true successors to Noke's original fancy lines.

Commemorative Wares

The Victorian and Edwardian (and later) obsession with recording significant events to do with Royalty, politics, war, or "The first of ...", was catered for by the production of a ceramic piece about the event. Doulton's wares typify the better souvenirs produced by the ceramic industry. In some cases they relate directly to events in New Zealand, eg. the vases/dishes commemorating the death of R. J. Seddon, the mugs/cups/plates produced specifically for firms such as D.I.C. or John Bates, for retail during the Canterbury Jubilee celebrations of 1900, or the New Zealand International Exhibition of Art and Industry in 1906-7. In Australia, John Shorter commissioned a design commemorating the Federation of Australia in 1901.

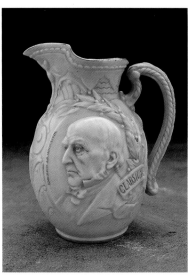

Parian-type slip-cast jug with vellum glaze, issued to commemorate the death of the Right Honourable William Ewart Gladstone, British Liberal politician and Prime Minister, 1898. Doulton & Co., Burslem. Height 19.7 cm. *Private Collection.*

Doulton's earliest commemorative dates to 1820 – a figural flask of Queen Caroline, George IV's estranged wife. Later Lambeth wares included figural and relief-moulded flasks, mugs, jugs and bottles depicting royalty, politicians, and heroic personalities such as Lord Nelson, Napoleon, H. M. Stanley, General Gordon and Christopher Colombus. With the expansion of the Lambeth Studios, commemoratives were made utilising the art pottery bodies and decorative techniques.

The closing years of Victoria's reign saw a number of moulded and coloured wares commemorating her Golden and Diamond Jubilees. Similar articles were produced for the coronations of all her successors up to the present, including a number for the never-crowned Edward VIII in 1936.

In a less solemn vein, two inkwells – one a grouchy and formidable female (known as "The Virago"), the other a baby with a bib – were designed by Leslie Harradine between 1905-8. Both are usually found bearing the inscription "Votes for Women", and were produced at the time of militant female agitation in England for the vote. "The Virago" certainly reflects the popular male bias against this movement, presumably to be reinforced every time a letter was written.

The Burslem factory also produced a range of commemorative wares, the earliest being an earthenware beaker for the Queen's Golden Jubilee in 1887. A limited number of special ones in fine bone china were made for presentation by Henry Doulton to the Queen, members of the Royal Family, the Archbishop of Canterbury, friends, important customers, and members of the Burslem staff; a similar version was made for the 1897 Diamond Jubilee. The range of commemoratives was similar to those produced at Lambeth, but on earthenware or bone china bodies, usually decorated by means of coloured transfers. The end of the Great War saw a number of Victory Wares, some issued as rack plates. Commemorative wares are issued to this day, usually in limited editions – a tradition begun in the 1930s with two-handled loving-cups and jugs.

Earthenware saucer commemorating the 1906 New Zealand International Exhibition of Art and Industry, showing the Exhibition Buildings at Christchurch. Royal Doulton, Burslem. Diameter 14 cm.
Canterbury Museum Collection.

Among those of interest in New Zealand were the souvenir mugs, tea sets and similar items produced for the Canterbury Jubilee in 1900, the New Zealand Exhibition of Art and Industry in 1906, and the death of Premier Richard John Seddon, also in 1906. Items were also

Bone china vase, *Mount Cook and Hookers Glacier*, hand-painted by Leonard Bentley, 1891-1901. Doulton & Co., Burslem. Height 18 cm. It is probable that this scene was copied from an engraving in an illustrated newspaper. It may well have been done to order. *Private Collection.*

produced for private individuals – for example, a dinner set ordered for the owner of the motor yacht, *Taranui*, built at Lyttelton in 1928.

New Zealand Wares

Also of particular interest to New Zealand collectors are those wares which have a local flavour. These are predominantly commemorative wares, as already discussed, or series wares, although one hand-painted vase by Leonard Bentley, featuring Mount Cook and the Hooker Glacier has recently been discovered.

A salt glazed stoneware range with applied medallions featuring tikis, tattooed faces and scrolls was introduced at the New Zealand International Exhibition in Christchurch in 1906. Known as Maori Ware and later, Kia Ora Ware (from the inscription on the scrolls), the designs were taken from illustrations by Augustus Hamilton in his *Maori Art,* published by the New Zealand Institute in 1901. These motifs were later produced in a range of stonewares with a mottled blue, brown or green ground (possibly emulating greenstone), and

Salt-glazed stoneware Maori Ware teapot (height 14.4 cm), bowl (diameter 13 cm), flagon (height 23.7 cm) and spill vase (height 15.8 cm), 1905-23. Royal Doulton, Burslem.
Auckland Museum and Institute Collection.

Maori Art tea-wares, c. 1926-40. Royal Doulton, Burslem. Teapot (height 14 cm), plate (diameter 15.5 cm), cup (height 5.6 cm), and saucer (diameter 13.4 cm).
Auckland Museum Collection (teapot);
Otago Museum Collection, Dunedin.

New Zealand thematic wares (left to right): Teapot with crackle glaze and frieze of kiwis, 1924-1940s, commissioned by John Bates & Co. of Christchurch and stamped accordingly (height 13 cm); earthenware teapot stand, issued for the Canterbury Jubilee Exhibition in 1900, the transfer prints illustrating Christchurch Anglican Cathedral, and John Robert Godley, so-called "Founder of Canterbury" (height 19.5 cm); bone china teapot with a photographic transfer portrait of Richard John Seddon, Premier of New Zealand, who died in 1906, *He stood for Empire* (height 11.5 cm). *Private Collections.*

included vases, flagons, jardinieres. steins and teapots. Although the later versions seem to have been better sellers, they are not perhaps as aesthetically satisfying as the original earthy beiges and browns.

In 1907 a special tea ware, featuring a Maori rafter pattern also adapted by Hamilton from traditional sources, was launched. Maori Art Ware was produced originally in bone china, with the design in red and black on a white ground. In 1928 an earthenware version was introduced, and a yellow or orange ground was also available. The pattern was also used as a border for rack plates featuring photographic reproductions of a Maori mother and child, a sheep farmer with his flock, various New Zealand landscapes, and a World War One soldier.

John Bates of Christchurch commissioned a special teapot with a band of kiwis in a frieze around the centre. The ground has a deliberately crazed effect. Introduced in 1924, the design was withdrawn during the 1940s, and although ordered in some quantity by Bates, does not appear to have had a great deal of popularity. A slightly more realistic kiwi in a bush setting featured on rack plates and a teapot in a short-lived series of wares which were in production between 1928 and 1939.

A specially-shaped ashtray featuring a map of New Zealand in blue and white was introduced in 1938 and appears to have been withdrawn during the Second World War. Two designs featuring New Zealand and City of Wellington crests are found on miniature vases, a teapot and a milk jug. These appear to date from about 1909.

Photographic scenes of Maori women by a hot pool, Lake Fergus and Mount Egmont (Taranaki) were used on rack plates, and were in production between 1939 and 1975.

Salt-glazed stoneware moulded figurine group, *The Race*, designed (but not signed) by George Tinworth, with assistance from Emily J. Partington, 1880-91. Doulton & Co., Lambeth. Height 13 cm.

This is an unrecorded group, although the frog has been found separately. *Private Collection.*

Figures

The production of Doulton figures had begun in Lambeth with George Tinworth who produced numerous small ceramic figures – mainly of children and comical groups of small animals such as mice and frogs. Other Lambeth artists, such as John Broad and Leslie Harradine, were also noted for their sculptural work which was often designed, as were a number of Tinworth's, for reproduction. However, it is to the Burslem factory that credit must go for the establishment of a commercially-successful figure tradition.

Charles Noke at Burslem began to experiment with figures in the 1890s. Slip-cast in a parian-type medium, with a particular parchment glaze known as "vellum", they were first shown at the Chicago

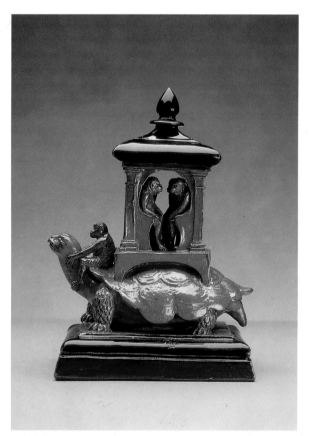 

Left: Salt-glazed moulded stoneware ornament, monkeys in a palanquin on a tortoise, by George Tinworth assisted by Florrie Jones, 1880-91. Doulton & Co., Lambeth. Height 17 cm. *Collection: Museum of Applied Arts and Sciences, Sydney, Australia.*
Right: Salt-glazed moulded figurine, *Organist*, Merry Musicians series by George Tinworth, 1902-13. Royal Doulton, Lambeth. Height 13.4 cm. *Collection: Museum of Applied Arts and Sciences, Sydney, Australia.*

Left: Terracotta press-moulded figurine, *Diana*, by John Broad, c. 1880. Doulton & Co., Lambeth. Height 29.7 cm.
Collection: Museum of Applied Arts and Sciences, Sydney, Australia.
Right: Parian-type slip-cast figurine, Lily Langtry or Sarah Bernhardt as *Cleopatra*, with tinted vellum glaze, modelled by Charles Noke, c. 1892. Height 31.3 cm. This is one of only two known copies. It was acquired by John Bates of Christchurch in the early 1900s, and sold at the N.Z.I.E., 1906. *Private Collection.*

Exhibition of 1892-3. Typically of Noke's literary interests, some were of Shakespearian characters, with the great contemporary acting duo of Sir Henry Irving and Ellen Terry shown in the roles of *Cardinal Wolsey* and *Queen Catherine,* from Shakespeare's, *Henry VIII.*

These and several others – *Shakespeare*, *A Moorish Minstrel,* and an enigmatic *Cleopatra* – were included in the 1906 Christchurch Exhibition. *Cleopatra* is believed by the family which acquired it at the Exhibition to have been a representation of renowned French actress Sarah Bernhardt.

The "divine Sarah" had appeared in a play by Sardou, *Cléopâtre,* which was written mainly as a vehicle for her remarkable dramatic techniques – following the climax of a performance in London in 1892, during which Cleopatra had stabbed a servant, totally destroyed the furnishings of her palace and collapsed in hysterics amongst the wreckage, a middle-aged matron is reported to have remarked (with great complacency), "How different, how very different from the home life of our own dear Queen!" Unfortunately for the Bernhardt-inspired figurine theory, production photographs bear virtually no resemblance to the Noke figure (of which only two are known to exist).

However, a recent discovery in an edition of Shakespeare's works, published by Collins in about 1900 and illustrated with photo-engravings of "eminent histrionic artists", suggests a more likely contender – professional beauty and sometime mistress of the Prince of Wales, the actress Lily Langtry, who appeared in *Antony and Cleopatra* in London (also in 1892). Certainly her profile, physique and above all her costume more nearly resemble the Doulton figure. It would seem likely, too, that Charles Noke, imbued with a passionate love of his English literary and dramatic heritage, would choose to depict (as he had with Ellen Terry) an English actress in a role by the most famous of English playwrights.

The motivation behind the production of figures was to bring about a renaissance of the Staffordshire figure-making tradition. Many of the figures produced in 19th century Staffordshire had been of dubious aesthetic quality, often poorly imitating 18th century material. Several of the factories involved had gone bankrupt.

The vellum figures were not very well-received – while the strength of the modelling was acknowledged, the ivory colour with subtle hints

Left: Slip-cast figurine, *Salome* H.N.1775, by Richard Garbe, R.A., issued in 1933 as a limited edition of 100, and sold out by 1939. Royal Doulton, Burslem. Height 20 cm. The artist may have been inspired by the first public performance of Oscar Wilde's play, *Salome*, banned since 1893. *Collection: Museum of Applied Arts and Sciences, Sydney, Australia.*

Right: Slip-cast sculpture, *West Wind* H.N.1776, by Richard Garbe, R.A., introduced in 1933 as a limited edition of 25, and sold out by 1939. Royal Doulton, Burslem. Height 36.8 cm. The sculpture was possibly inspired by Shelley's, *Ode to the West Wind.* *Museum of New Zealand Te Papa Tongarewa.*

Slip-cast figurines: *Digger (New Zealand)* H.N.321 (height 28.5 cm), *Blighty* (Great Britain) H.N.323 (height 29.2 cm), *Digger (Australia)* H.N.322 (height 28.5 cm), by Ernest W. Light, 1918-38.
This trio of World War I soldiers were modelled towards the end of the War. The Australian *Digger* was a portrait of John Austin Shorter, second son of the Shorter family of Sydney, who had been Doulton's agents for Australia since 1879. *Blighty* has a Titanian glaze finish. *Private Collections.*

of pale pink and green and delicate gilding, was not to the public taste. Noke therefore proceeded cautiously. Not relying entirely on the skills of the Doulton artists, he also explored a collaboration with various contemporary sculptors and modellers such as Phoebe Stabler, R. A., E. W. Light and William White. Later partnerships were established with Richard Garbe and Raoh Schorr.

One of the artists whose name became virtually synonymous with Royal Doulton figurines was Leslie Harradine, a brilliant young modeller who had worked for Doulton at Lambeth from 1902-12. While there he had produced models of a number of Dickens' characters – Pickwick, Sairey Gamp, Pecksniff, Mr Squeers, Micawber, The Fat Boy, and Sam Weller – as well as a bust of Dickens himself. These appealed greatly to Noke who had a profound love of Dickens' work. Following the Great War, Harradine agreed to supply Noke with figures, modelled at

Slip-cast stoneware "Dickens" figures by Leslie Harradine: *Sairey Gamp* (height 19.8 cm), *Mr Squeers* (height 23.5 cm), *Mr Pickwick* H19 (height 22 cm), *Mr Pecksniff* H21 (height 23cm), all c. 1913. Royal Doulton Lambeth. *Private Collections.*

Slip-cast figurine, *The Goosegirl*, by Leslie Harradine; in production 1921-38. Royal Doulton, Lambeth. Height 19.5 cm.

This bone china version has lost its H.N. number, but is similar to H.N.437 (earthenware). It was probably inspired by the German fairy story, told by the brothers Grimm, of the Princess who is made to change places with her maid, and become a goosegirl. *Private Collection.*

home, for potential reproduction in bone china. This association continued for nearly forty years. Among his most famous figures were *The Goose Girl*, *The Balloon Seller*, and *Top o' the Hill*. Versions of this last figure were presented to New Zealanders Edmund Hillary and George Lowe after their successful ascent of Mt. Everest in 1953.

Although the majority of creative artists associated with the Burslem factory have been men, two of the major figure sculptors have been women – Margaret (Peggy) Davies and Mary Nicoll.

Peggy Davies, a Burslem-born artist, studied at the Burslem College of Art, having won a scholarship there at the age of 12. For a short period of time she worked for Clarice Cliff, and then went to Doulton, as an assistant to Cecil Noke. She established herself as an independent artist following the Second World War and, like Harradine, for over thirty years supplied the firm with a steady stream of figures for reproduction. Her group, *The Marriage of Art and Industry*, designed in consultation with Director Design Jo Ledger, was the centre-piece of the Doulton stand at the 1958 Brussels International Exhibition. She succeeded Harradine in the tradition of the "Fair Ladies" which have become almost the trademark of Royal Doulton figurines.

Mary Nicoll, who died at the relatively young age of 52, was another independent artist, supplying figures to the company. Her work was particularly noted for its robust portrayal of characters such as *The Wayfarer, The Boatman, The Judge,* and *Tuppence a Bag* – the old "Bird Lady" from the film of P. L. Travers' much-loved children's book, *Mary Poppins.*

Today the ceramic figure tradition is continued by a number of younger artists, working independently or directly from Burslem. These include Pauline Parsons, Robert Jefferson, Peter Gee and Amanda Dixon.

The HN series of figures (the initials preceding the number which identifies each design, are those of Harry Nixon, who worked closely with Charles Noke in the development of the range) was launched in 1913, and continues to this day. The Doulton figures have had great appeal to the public, and today are almost the sole representatives of the greater decorative Doulton tradition. Again they signify the successful blending of good design and production, and commercial viability. The figures have provided a means for people to have well-produced but relatively-inexpensive examples of sculpture in their homes, and like the series ware and high-quality hand-painted pieces, have been a reflection of contemporary taste.

Slip-cast figurine [W.S.Penley as], *Charley's Aunt,* by Albert Toft, c. 1913. Royal Doulton, Burslem. Height 17.7 cm. This version has no H.N. number and was probably a special order of H.N.35. *Private Collection.*

Left: Slip-cast figurine, *Butterfly* H.N.719, by Leslie Harradine; in production 1925-38. Royal Doulton, Burslem. Height 16.5 cm. *Private Collection.*
Right: Slip-cast figurine, *The Sentimental Pierrot* H.N.36, by Charles Noke; in production 1918-38. Royal Doulton, Burslem. Height 13.9 cm. *Private Collection.*

Left: Slip-cast figurine group, *Fisherwomen*, by Charles Noke, c. 1917. Royal Doulton, Burslem. Height 29.5 cm. This piece has no H.N. number but is clearly related to a design for H.N.80. It is the second-only known example and is a unique colourway. There were many popular Victorian paintings based on the theme of fisherwomen awaiting the return of the boats. However, it is possible that Noke, a great admirer of Dickens, may have been inspired by the "storm scene" at Yarmouth, in *David Copperfield*, with its distraught fisherwomen on the beach. *Private Collection.*

Right: Slip-cast figurine group, *Young Mother with Child* H.N.1301, artist unrecorded. Royal Doulton, Burslem. Height 38 cm.
   Although this piece is believed to have been in production between 1928 and 1938, to date this is the only known example. It may have been inspired by one of the popular paintings of Augustus Johns of gypsy women. *Private Collection.*

Left: Slip-cast figurine, *King Charles* H.N.2084, by Charles Noke and Harry Tittensor; this version in production 1952-92. Royal Doulton, Burslem. Height 42.5 cm. *Private Collection.*
Right: Slip-cast figurines, *The Chelsea Pair (Female)* H.N.577 and *The Chelsea Pair (Male)* H.N.579, by Leslie Harradine; in production 1923-38. Royal Doulton, Burslem. Height 15.2 cm. During the 1920s there was a revival of interest in the products of the 18th century Chelsea factory, and a number of Doulton figurines of the period show this influence. *Private Collection.*

 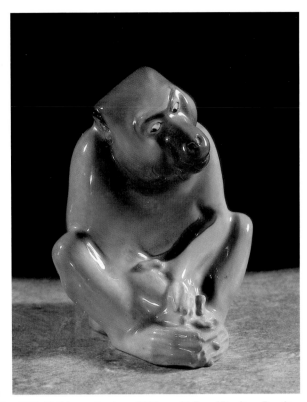

Left: Slip-cast figurine, *Fox in Red Hunting Coat* H.N.100; in production 1913-42, this version has a 1939 mould. Royal Doulton, Burslem. Height 15.5 cm. *Private Collection.*
Right: Slip-cast figurine, *Baboon* H.N.140, mould 147, date stamped 1917. Royal Doulton, Burslem. Height 15 cm.
 To date, this is the only known example of this figurine. *Private Collection.*

Polychrome stoneware finials, *Duck* (height 46 cm) and *Crow* (height 48.5 cm), by Gilbert Bayes, c. 1937. Royal Doulton, Lambeth.

 Gilbert Bayes was one of the most prominent British sculptors of the early 20th century. He produced a huge number of public pieces, believing strongly that decorative sculpture had a role in improving the environment.

 Bayes was commissioned in the 1930s by the St. Pancras Housing Association to create a number of colourful exterior-wall plaques and finials, such as these, for the washing line posts in the drying areas of housing estates. These were manufactured by Royal Doulton, with whom Bayes was associated from 1923 to 1939. *Dunedin Public Art Gallery.*

Left: Salt-glazed moulded toby jug, *The Man on a Barrel*; design registered in 1863, this version 1891-1901. Doulton & Co., Lambeth. Height 31 cm. *Private Collection.*
Right: Toby jug, *Charlie*, c. 1918. Royal Doulton, Burslem. Height 28 cm. A portrait of the greatest of the silent screen stars, Charlie Chaplin, this toby is in the style of the very early jugs where the removable hat formed a drinking vessel. *Private Collection.*

Character and Toby Jugs

The Toby Jug was an eighteenth century Staffordshire tradition, which within a few years of its appearance became the most popular jug ever produced in human likeness. Versions were produced at Lambeth, but those at Burslem have extended the design concept. Amongst the most unusual (and rare) is the 1918 jug, *Charlie,* which depicts comedian Charlie Chaplin in his most famous role, the Little Tramp. Copyright restrictions in the United States of America saw an almost immediate withdrawal of this figure, and it is only in recent years that examples of the small quantity produced have been found.

The production of the Character Jugs dates from 1934, and followed Noke's success with the figures. They are also in the Toby Jug tradition. Noke's idea was to extend the design range of the basic Toby to encompass a number of whimsical "characters" based in English song, literature, legend and history. By emphasising the head and shoulders, Noke was able to extend the possibilities of the traditional Toby. Other names associated with the Character Jug range besides Noke have been Harry Fenton, Leslie Harradine, David Biggs, Garry Sharpe and Max Henk.

The first two in the range were *John Barleycorn* and *Old Charley*. The latter depicts a nightwatchman in the days before the creation of the modern police force. They were established in the reign of Charles II, hence the nickname.

Left: Character jugs: *Granny* (early "toothless" version), designed by Harry Fenton and in production 1935-83 (height 14 cm); *John Barleycorn* (early version with handle leading inside jug), designed by Charles Noke, and in production 1934-9 (height 13.9 cm); and *Old Charley* designed by Charles Noke and in production 1934-83 (height 14 cm). *Private Collection.*

Right: The Maori, character jug. Royal Doulton, Burslem. 1939. This is a pilot or prototype jug. It was one of about six made in the Doulton Studio, and was sent to Australian Doulton agents, John Shorter Pty. Ltd. in 1939, for approval. The Second World War intervened and it was never put into production. *Private Collection.*

Old Charley's job was to patrol the streets, calling out the weather and the time of night. The sly wink which adorns his memorable face was undoubtedly induced by some of the strange goings-on which he saw on his nightly rounds. His traditional cry of, "All's well", could be said to sum up the success story of this and many other decorative products of the Doulton ceramic tradition.

Select Bibliography

– *Charles Dickens – A Tribute in Pottery.* Doulton & Co., Royal Doulton Pottery, Burslem

– *Dickens "Doultonised".* Royal Doulton Potteries, Burslem

– *Doulton & Co.Ltd – A Description of their Works and Manufactures, London, 1900.* Lambeth Pottery, London

– *Pictures in Pottery.* Royal Doulton Potteries, Lambeth, London

– *Royal Doulton Potteries.* Doulton & Co. Ltd., London

Atterbury, Paul and Irvine, Louise, 1979. *The Doulton Story: A Souvenir Booklet Produced Originally for the Exhibition held at the Victoria and Albert Museum, London, 30 May -12 August 1979.* Royal Doulton Tableware Ltd., Stoke-on-Trent

Betteridge, Margaret, 1979. *Royal Doulton Exhibition 1979.* Museum of Applied Arts and Sciences, Sydney

Blacker, J. F., 1917. *Fairyland on China.* Reprinted from *The Sphere,* February 1917. Royal Doulton Potteries, Burslem

Blacker, J. F., n.d. *"Sung" Glaze Ware.* The Royal Doulton Potteries, Burslem

Blacker, J. F., n.d. *Doulton's Burslem Wares.* Reprinted from *The Connoisseur Magazine,* Parts 1 & 2. Royal Doulton Potteries, Burslem

Blacker, J. F., n.d. *The Royal Doulton Potteries, Burslem, England.*

Dawson, Aileen, 1982. *Bernard Moore: Master Potter 1850-1935.* Richard Dennis, London

Eyles, Desmond, 1975. *The Doulton Lambeth Wares.* Hutchinson & Co. (Publishers) Ltd, London

Eyles, Desmond, 1980. *The Doulton Burslem Wares.* Barrie & Jenkins/Royal Doulton, London

Eyles, Desmond, Dennis, Richard, and Irvine, Louise, 1987. *Royal Doulton Figures.* Royal Doulton Limited, Stoke-on-Trent, and Richard Dennis, London

Gosse, Edmund (ed. Eyles, Desmond), 1970. *Sir Henry Doulton: The Man of Business as a Man of Imagination.* Hutchinson & Co. (Publishers) Ltd., London

Irvine, Louise, 1980. *Royal Doulton Series Ware, Volume 1.* Richard Dennis, London

Irvine, Louise, 1984. *Royal Doulton Bunnykins Collectors Book.* Richard Dennis, London

Irvine, Louise, 1984. *Royal Doulton Series Ware, Volume 2.* Richard Dennis, London

Irvine, Louise, 1986. *Royal Doulton Series Ware, Volume 3.* Richard Dennis, London

Irvine, Louise, 1988. *Royal Doulton Series Ware, Volume 4.* Richard Dennis, London

Lukins, Jocelyn, 1989. *Collecting Royal Doulton Character & Toby Jugs.* (2nd edition). Venta Books, London

Lukins, Jocelyn, n.d. *Doulton for the Collector.* PWC Publishing Ltd., Burton upon Trent

Lukins, Jocelyn, n.d. *Doulton Kingsware Whisky Flasks.* M. P. E., Yelverton

Owen, William, 1910. *The Royal Doulton Artists.* Royal Doulton Potteries, Burslem

Rose, Arthur V., n.d. *Discovery of a Long Lost Art.*

Rose, Peter, 1982. *George Tinworth.* C. D. N.Corporation, Los Angeles

Rose, Peter, 1985. *Hannah Barlow: A Doulton Artist.* Richard Dennis, London

Shorter, John Senr., 1932. *The John Slater Collection of Doulton Pottery. Technical Education Series No. 29,* Sydney Technological Museum. Government Printer, Sydney

Sparkes, John, 1874. *Some Recent Inventions and Applications of Lambeth Stoneware, Terra Cotta, and Other Pottery, for Internal and External Decoration. Journal of the Society of Arts,* 1 May 1874

CourierPost New Zealand Royal Doulton Exhibition 1992-93

Unless noted, all items were exhibited anonymously. The numbering system used here may vary from the order in which the items were exhibited. All content entries have been recorded in the following manner:

- **Description of the item and date**
- **Dimension** measured in centimetres. Kingswares, figurines, character jugs and series wares which are well-documented (see Bibliography), have not had measurements recorded.
- **Artist/Designer/Assistant**
- **Description of body and decorative technique/glazing process**
- **Name of manufacturing pottery**
- **Owner** (where applicable); **museum catalogue number** (where applicable).

    L = the Doulton Lambeth pottery
    B = the Doulton Burslem pottery

Lambeth Doulton Utilitarian Wares

L1 **Spigot for a storage or chemical jar, 1850s**
Height: 20.5cm; width: 17cm; length: 43cm
Salt-glazed stoneware. Doulton & Co., Lambeth.
Museum of Applied Arts and Sciences, Sydney, Australia.
91/2011

L2 **Water filter case, 2 gallon capacity, 1850s**
Height: 38cm; diameter: 28.5 max.cm
Salt-glazed stoneware; applied medallions. Doulton &
Watts, Lambeth.

Lambeth Doulton Decorated Utilitarian Wares

L3 **Spirit flask, *Lord Brougham*, c. 1832**
Height: 19cm
Salt-glazed stoneware, moulded in two parts with relief
decoration and the rims dipped in a darker glaze.
Doulton & Watts, Lambeth.
O'Neill Collection.

L4 **Spirit flask, *Mr & Mrs Caudle*, c. 1850**
Height: 19cm
Salt-glazed stoneware, moulded in two parts with relief
decoration and the rims dipped in a darker glaze.
Doulton & Watts, Lambeth.
O'Neill Collection.

L5 **Spirit flask, *The Triumph of the Pen*, c. 1850**
Height: 18cm; diameter: 10.4cm
Salt-glazed stoneware, moulded in two parts with relief
decoration and the rims dipped in a darker glaze.
Doulton & Watts, Lambeth.
Museum of Applied Arts and Sciences, Sydney, Australia.
A3872

L6 **Hunting Ware jug with a silver rim, 1903**
Height: 14.3cm; diameter: 14.7 max.cm
Salt-glazed stoneware, the top dipped in a darker glaze.
Royal Doulton, Lambeth.
Canterbury Museum Collection. EC178.57

L7 ***Bacchus* jug, 1880-1891**
Height: 18cm; diameter: 19.3 max.cm
Designer: **John Broad** (1880)
Assistants: Mary Goode, Agnes S. Horne
Salt-glazed stoneware, the top dipped in a darker glaze.
Doulton, Lambeth.

L8 **Water filter, 1885**
Height: 33cm
Assistants: Laura Green, Kate E. Russell, Florence
Bowditch, Ada Mayerek, Eborah Bissmire
Silicon Ware (stoneware), moulded and hand-applied
sprigs. Doulton & Co., Lambeth.
Walter C. Cook Decorative Art Collection, Museum of New
Zealand Te Papa Tongarewa.

L9 ***Isobath* inkstand, 1880s**
Height: 16.3cm; diameter: 17 max.cm
Assistant: Emily J. Partington ?
Salt-glazed stoneware; carved, applied beading. Doulton
& Co., Lambeth.

Lambeth Doulton Wares (Art Pottery)

L10 **Self-portrait medallion, 1895**
Height: 15.5cm; diameter: 13cm
Artist: **George Tinworth**
Assistants: Two unidentified
Press-moulded terracotta. Doulton & Co., Lambeth.
Museum of Applied Arts and Sciences, Sydney, Australia.
A7101

L11 **Flagon with leafy scrolls, 1869-72**
Height: 20cm; diameter: 14.5cm
Artist: **George Tinworth**
Salt-glazed stoneware; incised, carved, applied beading.
Doulton & Co., Lambeth.
Sir Henry Doulton Gallery, Royal Doulton (UK) Ltd. LF20

L12 **Jardinière with elephant supports, 1876-80**
Height: 19.7cm; diameter: 25cm
Artist: **George Tinworth**
Assistant: William Hollowell ?
Salt-glazed stoneware; moulded figurines, incised,
carved, applied beading. Doulton & Co., Lambeth.

L13 **Lemonade jug with leafy scrolls and silver rim, 1881**
Height: 24.1cm; diameter: 15.5 max.cm
Artist: **George Tinworth**
Assistant: Fanny Clark
Salt-glazed stoneware; carved, applied beading. Doulton
& Co., Lambeth.

L14 **Two-handled vase with amorini, owls, and foliage,
1876**
Height: 65cm; diameter: 26.5 max.cm
Artists: **George Tinworth, Eliza Simmance**
Assistant: Miss L. Goldsack
Salt-glazed stoneware; moulded figurines, incised, with
applied beading. Doulton & Co. Lambeth.
Museum of Applied Arts and Sciences, Sydney, Australia.
87/779

L15 **Spill vase with leafy scrolls and two mice, 1881**
Height: 13.5cm; diameter: 22.5 max.cm
Artist: **George Tinworth**
Assistant: Emma A. Burrows
Salt-glazed stoneware; moulded figurines, incised with
applied beading. Doulton & Co., Lambeth.
Manawatu Museum Society Incorporated. 82/75/70

L16 **Plaque, *And Behold the Angel of the Lord came upon
him*. [St.Peter in Prison] c. 1871**
Height: 9.5cm; width: 11.5cm
Artist: **George Tinworth**
Salt-glazed stoneware; modelled in high relief. This is
possibly a maquette for a larger work. A similar piece
was produced in 1871. Doulton & Co., Lambeth.
Museum of Applied Arts and Sciences, Sydney, Australia.
A3784

L17 **Jug with adult and young deer, 1871-2**
Height: 21.6cm
Artist: **Hannah Barlow**
Salt-glazed stoneware; incised. Doulton & Co., Lambeth.
Walter C. Cook Decorative Art Collection, Museum of New
Zealand Te Papa Tongarewa.

L18 Jug with frieze of hares, 1876
Height: 23.6cm; diameter: 13.5 max.cm
Artist: **Hannah Barlow**
Assistants: Emily E. Stormer, Annie Neal
Salt-glazed stoneware; incised with applied beading.
Doulton & Co., Lambeth.
Canterbury Museum Collection. E2150.0

L19 Nautilus shell vase, with sea horses and amorini, c. 1878
Height: 15.4cm; width: 12.7cm; length: 24.4cm
Artists:(attributed) **George Tinworth, Hannah Barlow**
Salt-glazed stoneware; moulded figurines, incised
through white slip, with applied beading. Doulton & Co.,
Lambeth.
*Museum of Applied Arts and Sciences, Sydney, Australia.
A3607*

L20 Lemonade jug with E.P.N.S. lid, and frieze of deer, 1882
Height: 26.5cm; diameter: 16 max.cm
Artist: **Hannah Barlow**
Assistants Lucy Barlow, Letitia Rosevear, Edith Green,
Harriett E. Hibbut
Salt-glazed stoneware; incised through white slip, incised
and coloured decoration with applied medallions.
Doulton & Co., Lambeth.

L21 Vase with donkeys and children, 1883
Height: 30.3cm; diameter: 13.5cm
Artist: **Hannah Barlow**
Assistant: Lucy Barlow
Salt-glazed stoneware, incised though white slip, incised
with applied beading. Doulton & Co., Lambeth.
*Museum of Applied Arts and Sciences, Sydney, Australia.
2838*

L22 Jug with leaf and floral medallion design, 1871-2
Height: 14.1cm; diameter: 12cm
Artist: **Arthur Barlow**
Salt-glazed stoneware; incised. Doulton & Co., Lambeth.
Auckland Museum. 277A

L23 Flagon with leaf and diagonal bands design, 1871-2
Height: 20cm; diameter: 13 max.cm
Artist: **Arthur Barlow**
Salt glazed stoneware; incised. Doulton & Co., Lambeth.
*Hawke's Bay Cultural Trust, Hawke's Bay Museum, Napier.
57/63/2*

L24 Vase with stylized flowers and foliage, 1881
Height: 35.4cm; diameter: 12cm
Artists: **Eliza Simmance, Elizabeth Atkins**
Assistants: Louisa Russell, Ellen Palmer, Ellen B. Smith
Salt-glazed stoneware; carved, *pâte-sur-pâte*, with applied
medallions. Doulton & Co., Lambeth.

L25 Mug with floral design, 1882-91
Height: 13.2cm
Artist: **Eliza Simmance**
Assistant: Jane Hurst
Salt-glazed stoneware; incised, with slip decoration.
Doulton & Co., Lambeth.
Art Gallery of New South Wales Collection. 2562

L26 Water jug with stylized poppies and foliage, 1882-91
Height: 21.5cm; diameter: 15 max.cm
Artist: **Arthur Pearce**
Assistant: Jane Hurst
Salt-glazed stoneware; carved with raised outlines.
Doulton & Co., Lambeth.
Art Gallery of New South Wales Collection. 2550

L27 Tobacco jar with leafy scrolls, 1882-91
Height: 13.5cm
Assistants: Annie Horton, Alice Cooke
Salt-glazed stoneware; moulded and applied medallions
on a textured ground produced by impressing discs.
Doulton & Co., Lambeth.

L28 Vase with fox, hen and rooster, 1882
Height: 46.7cm; diameter: 28.9cm
Artist: **Unsigned; previously attributed to ? W. or ? A.
Cund, but could be by Hannah Barlow**
Salt-glazed stoneware; full relief modelled figurines and
incised decoration. Doulton & Co., Lambeth.
*Museum of Applied Arts and Sciences, Sydney, Australia.
2830*

L29 Vase, pale yellow ground with fish and weeds, 1883
Height: 17cm; diameter: 21.5cm
Artist: **George Hugo Tabor**
Salt glazed stoneware, the glaze slightly lustred; relief
decoration. Doulton & Co., Lambeth.

L30 Vase with fish, dragonflies and irises on a lozenge ground, 1883
Height: 28.4cm; diameter: 16.7cm
Artist: **Harry Barnard**
Assistants: Charlotte Lamb ?, Ella H. Adams
Salt-glazed stoneware; carved, with applied modelled
medallions. Doulton & Co., Lambeth.
*Museum of Applied Arts and Sciences, Sydney, Australia.
2858*

L31 Vase with sparrows on a plum tree branch, 1883
Height: 42cm; diameter: 17.8cm
Artist: **Florence Barlow**
Assistants: Emma A. Burrows, Elizabeth J. Adams, Elsie
S. Thomas, Lucy Barlow
Salt-glazed stoneware; *pâte-sur-pâte* painting, incised,
carved, applied beading. Doulton & Co., Lambeth.

L32 Vase with raised foliage ground, and reserves of birds and foliage, 1883
Height: 31.8cm; diameter: 13.1cm
Artist: **Florence Barlow**
(Remaining marks obscured).
Salt-glazed stoneware; *pâte-sur-pâte* decoration. Doulton
& Co., Lambeth.
*Museum of Applied Arts and Sciences, Sydney, Australia.
2835*

L33 Vase with stippled ground, bird and grasses, 1883
Height: 36.9cm; diameter: 10cm
Artist: **Florence Barlow**
(Other marks obscured)
Salt-glazed stoneware; stippled ground and *pâte-sur-pâte*
decoration. Doulton & Co., Lambeth.
*Museum of Applied Arts and Sciences, Sydney, Australia.
2836*

L34 Vase with donkeys and birds, 1880-91
Height: 23cm; diameter: 10 max.cm
Artists: **Hannah Barlow, Florence Barlow**
Assistants: Louisa Ayling, Louisa Wakely, three
unidentified
Salt-glazed stoneware; incised and *pâte-sur-pâte*
decoration, with applied beading. Doulton & Co.,
Lambeth.
Art Gallery of New South Wales Collection. 2559

**L35 Vase, mottled neck and foot, outlined panels, and
reserves with birds and flowers, 1891-1901**
Height: 35.5cm; diameter: 15.5cm
Artist: **Florence Barlow**
Assistant: Bessie Newbery
Salt-glazed stoneware; tube-tooled outlines and *pâte-sur-pâte* decoration. Doulton & Co., Lambeth.
The late Herbert Mawdesley Bourne.

**L36 Jug, stippled ground, blue outlined wave panels, with
birds on a branch, 1891-1901**
Height: 24cm; diameter: 12.7cm
Artist: **Florence Barlow**
Assistants: Two, unidentified
Salt-glazed stoneware; tube-tooled outlines, stippled
ground and *pâte-sur-pâte* decoration. Doulton & Co.,
Lambeth.

**L37 Covered urn, with foliate designs, trellis and blossom,
Art Union of London prize, 1891-3**
Height: 29.2cm
Artist: **Eliza Simmance**
Assistants: Emily J. Partington, Louisa Russell
Salt-glazed stoneware; *pâte-sur-pâte*, carved and incised
coloured decoration, stippled ground. Doulton & Co.,
Lambeth.
*Walter C. Cook Decorative Art Collection, Museum of New
Zealand Te Papa Tongarewa.*

**L38 Vase with swirling stylized flowers, Art Union of
London prize, 1891-3**
Height: 34.3cm
Artist: **Eliza Simmance**
Assistants: Emily J. Partington, Louisa Russell
Salt-glazed stoneware; *pâte-sur-pâte*, carved and incised
decoration, stippled ground. Doulton & Co., Lambeth.
*Walter C. Cook Decorative Art Collection, Museum of New
Zealand Te Papa Tongarewa.*

**L39 Jug with stylized poppies in a frieze, mottled neck and
foot; Art Union of London prize, 1891-1901**
Height: 26.5cm; diameter: 10cm
Artist: **Mark V. Marshall**
Assistant: Fanny Sayers
Salt-glazed stoneware; motifs outlined by tube-tooling,
with applied beading. Doulton & Co., Lambeth.

L40 Vase with frieze of horses and trees, 1885
Height: 27cm; diameter: 26cm
Artist: **Hannah Barlow**
Assistants: Augusta M. Birnie ?
Salt-glazed stoneware; incised through white slip,
incised, carved with applied beading. Doulton & Co.,
Lambeth.

**L41a-b Pair of ewer vases, with friezes of standing and lying
cattle, 1887**
Height: 38.5cm; diameter: 15 max.cm
Artist: **Hannah Barlow**
Assistants: Louisa Russell, Miss A. Hays ?
Salt-glazed stoneware; incised through white slip,
incised, carved with applied beading. Doulton & Co.,
Lambeth.

L42 Vase with deer, 1887
Height: 16.8cm; diameter: 15cm
Artist: **Hannah Barlow**
Assistants: Alice E. Budden, Kate J. Castle, Bessie
Newbery
Salt-glazed stoneware; incised through white slip,
incised, carved with applied medallions. Doulton & Co.,
Lambeth.

L43 Vase with frieze of donkeys, 1891-1901
Height: 19.9cm; diameter: 13cm
Artist: **Hannah Barlow**
Assistants: Jane Hurst, Kate J. Castle, Miss A. Hays
Salt-glazed stoneware; incised through white slip,
incised, carved and coloured decoration. Doulton & Co.,
Lambeth.

**L44 Vase with stylized floral border and herd of deer, 1891-
1901**
Height: 44cm; diameter: 20.4cm
Artists: **Hannah Barlow, Eliza Simmance**
Assistant: Miss A. Hays
Salt-glazed stoneware; incised through white slip,
incised, carved, with applied beading. Doulton & Co.,
Lambeth.

**L45 Vase with mottled neck and foot, sinuous scrolls, and
frieze of kangaroos and tall grasses, 1897-1901**
Height: 44cm; diameter: 19.5cm
Artist: **Hannah Barlow**
Assistants: Rosina Brown, Alice M. Ritchin ?, one
unidentified
Salt-glazed stoneware; *pâte-sur-pâte*, and freely-painted
flat pigment. Doulton & Co., Lambeth.
Art Gallery of New South Wales Collection. 2568

**L46 Vase with mottled neck and foot, beading and
medallions, frieze of donkeys, 1913**
Height: 46cm; diameter: 18cm
Artist: **Hannah Barlow**
Assistants: Ethel Beard, Gladys Joyce
Salt-glazed stoneware; incised through white slip, with
coloured borders and applied beading. Royal Doulton,
Lambeth.

**L47a-b Pair of beakers with silver rims and foliate scrolls,
1880**
Height: 14cm; diameter: 8.5cm
Artist: **Emily E. Stormer**
Assistants: Mary Aitken, unidentified
Salt-glazed stoneware; incised and coloured foliage, with
pâte-sur-pâte flowers and meander patterning, applied
beading. Doulton & Co., Lambeth.

L48 **Tyg [3-handled cup] with a silver rim, stylized flowers and leafy sprays, 1880**
Height: 16.5cm; diameter: 14cm
Artist: **Edith Lupton**
Assistant: Edith Kemp
Salt-glazed stoneware; *pâte-sur-pâte* painting, incised applied beading. Doulton & Co., Lambeth.

L49 **Miniature biscuit barrel with E.P.N.S. lid and handle, stylized floral spays and leaves, 1881**
Height: 13cm; diameter: 11.4cm
Artist: **Edith Lupton**
Assistant: Alice Robjeant
Salt-glazed stoneware; incised and coloured decoration with applied beading and medallions. Doulton & Co., Lambeth.

L50 **Jardinière with stylized foliage, 1882**
Height: 24.5cm; diameter: 23cm
Artist: **Elizabeth Atkins**
Assistants: Kate J. Castle, Emma A. Burrows, three unidentified
Salt-glazed stoneware; carved, stippled ground, applied beading. Doulton & Co., Lambeth.

L51 **Candlestick with stylized foliage, 1880**
Height: 27cm; diameter (base): 12cm
Artist: **Emily E. Stormer**
Assistant: Eliza Bowen
Salt-glazed stoneware; incised *pâte-sur-pâte* ground, applied beading and medallions. Doulton & Co., Lambeth.

L52 **Vase with stylized foliage, 1883**
Height: 30.4cm; diameter: 14.3cm
Artist: **George Tinworth**
Assistants: Florence Dennis, Rosina Brown, Emma A. Burrows
Salt-glazed stoneware; incised, carved *pâte-sur-pâte* ground pattern, applied beading and medallions. Doulton & Co., Lambeth.
Museum of Applied Arts and Sciences, Sydney, Australia. 2845

L53 **Vase with leafy scrolls and beading, mottled inner neck and foot, 1891-1901**
Height: 27.5cm; diameter: 10.5 max.cm
Artist: **George Tinworth**
Assistants: Emma A. Burrows, unidentified
Salt-glazed stoneware; incised *pâte-sur-pâte* honey-comb ground pattern, applied beading and medallions. Doulton & Co., Lambeth.

L54 **Candlestick in the form of an oak tree, supported by a bear and its cub, 1880**
Height: 22.5cm; diameter: 12.3cm
Artist: **Mary Ann Thomson**
Salt-glazed stoneware; high relief modelling and incised decoration. Doulton & Co., Lambeth.
Museum of Applied Arts and Sciences, Sydney, Australia. 189a

L55 **Dish in form of a Viking ship with a sea serpent, 1880-91**
Height: 18.2cm; length: 28.5cm; width: 17.3cm
Artists: **Mark V. Marshall, Mary Ann Thomson ?**
Assistant: Lizzie Padbury
Salt-glazed stoneware; modelled and pierced decoration. Doulton & Co., Lambeth.
Museum of Applied Arts and Sciences, Sydney, Australia. A3742

L56 **Vase with Persian-style flowers and leaves, mottled neck, 1885**
Height: 32cm; diameter: 20.4cm
Artist: **Frank Butler**
Assistants: Rosina Brown, Ernest Bishop
Salt-glazed stoneware; carved, applied beading. Doulton & Co., Lambeth.

L57 **Vase with reserves of stippled ground and floral sprays, and foliage, 1886**
Height: 35.7cm; diameter: 23cm
Artist: **Eliza Simmance**
Assistants: Annie Neal, Alice Longhurst, Catherine Francis ?
Salt-glazed stoneware; *pâte-sur-pâte*, carved and applied beading. Doulton & Co., Lambeth.

L58 **Vase with mottled neck, trellis reserves, and reserves with formal floral sprays, 1887**
Height: 31.5cm; diameter: 15.3cm
Assistants: Edith M. Coleman, Mary Aitken
Salt-glazed stoneware; *pâte-sur-pâte*, incised, pierced strapwork; applied beading. Doulton & Co., Lambeth.
The late Herbert Mawdesley Bourne.

L59 **Vase *Fire and Art*, 1889**
Height: 32cm; diameter: 15 max.cm
Artist: **Mark V. Marshall**
Salt-glazed stoneware; modelled in high and low relief, incised. [Although it does not have a Doulton backstamp, the vase is signed and dated, and bears all the hallmarks of a Doulton & Co., Lambeth product.]
City Museum & Art Gallery, Stoke-on-Trent, England. 4333

L60 **Bowl with waves and fish, 1891-1901**
Height: 11.5cm; diameter: 32 max.cm
Artist: **Mark V. Marshall**
Salt-glazed stoneware; thrown and pulled at rim; modelled in low-relief. Doulton & Co., Lambeth.
City Museum & Art Gallery, Stoke-on-Trent, England. 461.P35

L61 **Candlestick with lizard-like creature, 1880-91**
Height: 19cm; diameter (base): 10cm
Artist: **Mark V. Marshall**
Assistants: Rosina Brown
Salt-glazed stoneware; relief modelling. Doulton & Co., Lambeth.

L62 **Vase with flared rim and relief foliage, 1891-2**
Height: 23cm; diameter: 10.5cm
Artist: **Mark V. Marshall**
Assistant Louisa Wakely
Salt-glazed stoneware; carved and incised. Doulton & Co., Lambeth.
Museum of Applied Arts and Sciences, Sydney, Australia. A3589

L63a-b **Pair of vases with sinuous flowers and foliage, 1902-1912**
Height: 30.5cm; diameter: 15cm
Artist: **Mark V. Marshall**
Salt-glazed stoneware; tube-tooled outlines and applied beading. Royal Doulton, Lambeth.

L64 **Vase with stylized flowers and seed pods, 1891-1901**
Height: 20.5cm; diameter: 14cm
Artist: **Frank Butler**
Salt-glazed stoneware; pulled and carved at the rim, carved, applied beading, *pâte-sur-pâte*. Doulton & Co., Lambeth.

L65 **Vase with stylized *Art Nouveau* tulips, 1903**
Height: 23cm; diameter: 15cm
Artist: **Eliza Simmance**
Assistant: Unidentified
Salt-glazed stoneware; freely-painted and tube-tooled outlines, *pâte-sur-pâte*. Royal Doulton, Lambeth.

L66 **Vase with *Art Nouveau* stylized flowers, 1902-14**
Height: 40cm; diameter: 15.3cm
Artist: **Eliza Simmance**
Assistants;   Jane Hurst, Emily L. Robinson ?
Salt-glazed stoneware; tube-tooled outlines, applied beading. Royal Doulton, Lambeth.

L67 **Vase with tulips, 1902**
Height: 46cm; diameter: 17.8cm
Artist: **Frank Butler**
Assistant: Rosina Brown
Salt-glazed stoneware; incised. Royal Doulton, Lambeth.

L68 **Vase with flared rim and relief foliage, 1902-12**
Height: 27.6cm; diameter: 8.9cm
Artist: **Mark V. Marshall**
Salt-glazed stoneware; carved. Royal Doulton, Lambeth.

L69 **Vase with dragon or lizard-like creature, 1902-12**
Height: 27.6cm; diameter: 12.9cm
Artist: **Mark V. Marshall**
Salt-glazed stoneware; carved in low-relief. Royal Doulton, Lambeth.
Museum of Applied Arts and Sciences, Sydney, Australia. A3842

L70 **Jardinière and pedestal with *Art Nouveau* flowers and leaves, 1902-15**
Height: 123cm
Artist: **Unmarked**
Assistants: Unidentified
Salt-glazed stoneware; tube-tooled outlines, applied beading. Royal Doulton, Lambeth.

L71 **Vase with flowers and foliage, c. 1930**
Height: 18.5cm; diameter: 16.7cm
Artist: **Vera Huggins**
Salt-glazed stoneware; incised. Royal Doulton, Lambeth.
Museum of Applied Arts and Sciences, Sydney, Australia. A4312-1

L72 **Vase with "Persian" floral frieze, 1922-7**
Height: 54.5cm; diameter: 30cm
Artist: **Harry Simeon**
Salt-glazed stoneware; incised and slip painted. Royal Doulton, Lambeth.

L73 **Vase with vertical stylized foliage, 1922-7**
Height: 23cm; diameter: 9cm
Artist: **Harry Simeon**
Salt-glazed stoneware; incised. Royal Doulton, Lambeth.
Hawke's Bay Cultural Trust, Hawke's Bay Museum, Napier. 57/63/1

L74 **Vase with peacock and foliage, c. 1930**
Height: 29cm; diameter: 13.4cm
Artist: **Vera Huggins**
Salt-glazed stoneware; incised and slip painted. Royal Doulton, Lambeth.
Sir Henry Doulton Gallery, Royal Doulton (UK) Ltd. LF11

L75 **Vinegar or oil flask, 1952-6**
Height: 20cm; diameter: 7.5cm
Designer: **Agnete Hoy**
Assistant: Unidentified
Salt-glazed stoneware; painted underglaze. Royal Doulton, Lambeth.
Sir Henry Doulton Gallery, Royal Doulton (UK) Ltd. LF7

L76 **Pair of whisky tumblers, leaf and horizontal line patterns, 1952-6**
Height: 5.5cm; diameter: 4cm
Artist: **Agnete Hoy**
Salt-glazed stoneware; incised. Royal Doulton, Lambeth.

L77 **Lamp base with floral design, 1952-6**
Height: 17cm; diameter: 14cm
Artist: **Agnete Hoy**
Salt-glazed stoneware; underglaze painted, incised. Royal Doulton, Lambeth.
Sir Henry Doulton Gallery, Royal Doulton (UK) Ltd. LF2

L78 **Lambeth Faience vase, orange-red ground with red and white Erica flowers, 1891-1901**
Height: 28.5cm; diameter: 10.5cm
Artist: **Katherine B. Smallfield**
Earthenware; underglaze painted. Royal Doulton, Lambeth.
Museum of Applied Arts and Sciences, Sydney, Australia. A837/1

L79 **Lambeth Faience vase with Sturt's Desert Pea flowers, 1891-1902**
Height: 20cm; diameter: 17cm
Artist: **Katherine B. Smallfield**
Earthenware; underglaze painted. Royal Doulton, Lambeth.
Museum of Applied Arts and Sciences, Sydney, Australia. A840/2

L80a-b **Pair of Lambeth Faience vases with yellow irises on a blue ground, 1891-1914**
Height: 27.5cm; diameter: 13.8cm
Artist: Unknown
Earthenware; underglaze painted. Royal Doulton, Lambeth.

L81 **Lambeth Faience vase with dark blue bands, vertical arrangement of yellow and purple irises on a pale blue ground, 1898-1913**
Height: 35cm; diameter: 17 max.cm
Artist: **Emily J. Gillman**
Earthenware; underglaze painted. Royal Doulton, Lambeth.

L82 **Lambeth Faience vase with fairy and white butterflies on a blue ground, grapes and leaves around neck, 1891-1901**
Height: 26cm; diameter: 12cm
Artist: **Margaret E. Thompson**
Assistant: Minnie Webb
Earthenware; underglaze painted. Doulton & Co., Lambeth.
Art Gallery of New South Wales Collection. 2025

L83 **Lambeth Faience vase with vertical straps enclosing panels of yellow tulips, 1874-77**
Height: 18.2cm; diameter: 15.4cm
Artist: **Mary Butterton**
Earthenware; underglaze painted on a Pinder, Bourne blank. Doulton & Co., Lambeth.
Museum of Applied Arts and Sciences, Sydney, Australia. 2808

L84 **Lambeth Faience vase, *Orpheus,* on a Greek amphora shape, c. 1888**
Height: 34cm; diameter: 35cm ·
Artist: **John Eyre**
Earthenware; underglaze painted. Doulton & Co., Lambeth.
Sir Henry Doulton Gallery, Royal Doulton (UK) Ltd.

L85 **Impasto vase, brown flecked ground with white crocuses, 1879**
Height: 26cm; diameter: 12 max.cm
Artist: **Unidentified**
Earthenware; slip painted underglaze. Doulton & Co., Lambeth.

L86 **Impasto vase, ochre ground with blue hydrangeas, 1881**
Height: 19.1cm; diameter: 9.5cm
Artist: **Rosa Keen**
Assistant: Kate J. Castle ·
Earthenware; slip painted underglaze. Doulton & Co., Lambeth.

L87 **Impasto vase, green ground with cream daises and circular reserves with white blossom sprays, 1883**
Height: 36.6cm; diameter: 21.2cm
Artist: **Fannie J. Allen**
Earthenware; slip painted underglaze. Doulton & Co., Lambeth.
Museum of Applied Arts and Sciences, Sydney, Australia. 2819

L88 **Silicon Ware vase with geometric decoration, 1882**
Height: 40.9cm; diameter: 14.4cm
Artist: **Edith Lupton**
Assistant: Rosetta Hazeldine
Stoneware; scalloped, perforated and incised, *pâte-sur-pâte* decoration. Doulton & Co., Lambeth.
Museum of Applied Arts and Sciences, Sydney, Australia. 2859

L89 **Silicon Ware vase with geometric and floral designs, 1883**
Height: 31.6cm; diameter: 13.1cm
Artist: **Eliza Simmance**
Stoneware; stippled, perforated and incised, *pâte-sur-pâte* decoration. Doulton & Co., Lambeth.
Museum of Applied Arts and Sciences, Sydney, Australia. 2860

L90 **Silicon Ware and Doulton & Slater's Patent vase with sprays of pale blossom, and a collar of overlapping blue flowers, 1885** ˙
Height: 26cm; diameter: 14cm
Artist: **Eliza Simmance**
Stoneware; Doulton & Slater's Patent (Chiné) decoration, with *pâte-sur-pâte*. Doulton & Co., Lambeth.
Walter C. Cook Decorative Art Collection, Museum of New Zealand Te Papa Tongarewa.

L91 **Silicon Ware covered vase with applied blue, white and brown geometric medallions and bosses, 1882**
Height: 32cm; diameter: 19 max.cm
Assistant: Unidentified
Stoneware; brown ground, applied medallions. Doulton & Co., Lambeth.

L92 **Silicon Ware vase with applied medallions, leaf band, and gilded decoration, 1891-3**
Height: 16cm; diameter: 9cm
Assistant: Laura Gooderham
Stoneware; applied medallions, beading, gilded. Doulton & Co., Lambeth.

L93 **Black Leather Ware jug with a silver rim, *Bitter must be the Cup that a Smile will not Sweeten,* 1889-90**
Height: 17cm; diameter: 13.5cm
Artist: Unknown
Stoneware; Doulton & Slater's Patent ground; silver rim.

L94 [Shown at Canterbury Museum only]
Jardinière, electroplated with brass finish, six scenes from Classical mythology, 1890s
Height: 30cm; diameter: 30cm
Unsigned
Earthenware; copper-plated and "brassed". Impressed stamp DOULTON'S.

L95 **Natural Foliage Ware vase with fern leaves, 1891-2**
Height: 28cm; diameter: 11cm
Assistants: Fanny Sayers ?, Miss H. Toland ?, Elizabeth Shelley, Edith H. Woodington
Stoneware; impressed, underglaze painted. Doulton & Co., Lambeth.

L96 **Natural Foliage Ware jardinière, oak leaves, 1891-2**
Height: 20.5cm; diameter: 21.5cm
Assistants: Fanny Sayers ?
Stoneware; impressed, underglaze painted. Doulton & Co., Lambeth.

L97 **Natural Foliage Ware jug, 1886-91**
Height: 20.3cm; diameter: 12.4cm
Stoneware; impressed, underglaze painted. Doulton & Co., Lambeth.

L98 **Natural Foliage Ware beaker, 1886-91**
Height: 13.5cm; diameter: 8.5cm
Stoneware; impressed, underglaze painted. Doulton & Co., Lambeth.

L99 **Natural Foliage Ware teapot, c. 1910**
Height: 13.2cm; diameter: 15.7cm
Designer/Assistant: Maud Bowden
Stoneware; impressed, underglaze painted. Royal Doulton, Lambeth.
Museum of Applied Arts and Sciences, Sydney, Australia. A3806

L100   Carrara Ware ewer vase with "Persian style" foliage, 1887-91
Height: 20cm; diameter: 10cm
Artist: **Mark V. Marshall**
Assistants: Jessie Boyce ?, Miss S. Pearson, one unidentified
Stoneware; underglaze painted. Doulton & Co., Lambeth.
Art Gallery of New South Wales Collection. 2551

L101   Cararra Ware vase with large white and yellow daisies, 1891-1901
Height: 33cm; diameter: 15cm
Assistants: Miss K. Heywood, two unidentified
Stoneware; underglaze painted. Doulton & Co., Lambeth.

L102   Velluma Ware candlestick, with rural landscape, 1911-1914
Height: 22cm; diameter: 12cm
Designers: Arthur Pearce, William Rowe
Earthenware; glazed and transfer-printed. Royal Doulton, Lambeth.

L103   *The Race* , figurine group of a mouse and a frog on pennyfarthing bicycles, 1880-91
Height: 13cm; diameter: 10cm
Artist: **George Tinworth (unsigned)**
Assistant: Emily J. Partington
Salt-glazed stoneware; moulded. Doulton & Co., Lambeth.

L104   Ashtray in form of a life-saving ring with a man's head wearing a hat; inscription, *Saved*, c. 1878
Height: 7.5cm; diameter: 10cm
Designer: **Herbert Ellis**
Salt-glazed stoneware; moulded. Doulton & Co., Lambeth.

L105   Inkwell,*Votes for Women*, in form of woman in brown dress with a blue apron and with folded arms, c. 1905-8
Height: 9cm; diameter: 6.2cm
Designer: **Leslie Harradine**
Salt-glazed stoneware; moulded. Royal Doulton, Lambeth.
Alan Blakeman, N.B.M., S.Yorks.

L106   Inkwell,*The Baby* , in form of an infant with a wide-sleeved vest and a bib.
Height: 9cm; diameter: 6.2cm
Designer: **Leslie Harradine**
Salt-glazed stoneware; moulded. Royal Doulton, Lambeth.
Alan Blakeman, N.B.M., S.Yorks.

L107   Ornament, monkeys in a palanquin on a tortoise, 1880-1891.
Height: 17cm; length: 22.7cm; width: 10cm
Artist: **George Tinworth**
Assistant: Florrie Jones
Salt-glazed stoneware; moulded. Doulton & Co., Lambeth.
Museum of Applied Arts and Sciences, Sydney, Australia. A3918

L108   Doulton & Slater's Patent Ware biscuit barrel with E.P.N.S. lid and handle, dark brown ground with applied white daisies, 1885-91
Height: 13.3cm; diameter: 11.4cm
Assistant: Unidentified
Stoneware; impressed, moulded and applied sprigs. Doulton & Co., Lambeth.

L109   Doulton & Slater's Patent Ware vase, mottled brown slender neck with red and gold collar, round body with lace pattern; flowers picked out in white, red and gilt highlights, 1902-18
Height: 27cm; diameter: 13.5cm
Designed for mass production, artist unknown.
Assistants: Kate J. Castle ?, Annie Neal ?
Stoneware; impressed decoration, *pâte-sur-pâte*, gilded. Royal Doulton, Lambeth.

L110   Doulton & Slater's Patent Ware ewer vase, blue ground, red band at neck, flowers picked out in gold and white, enamelled turquoise flowers, 1891-1901
Height: 20.5cm; diameter: 8 max.cm
Artist: **L. Imogen Durtnall**
Stoneware; impressed, *pâte-sur-pâte*, gilded. Doulton & Co., Lambeth.
Art Gallery of New South Wales Collection. 2548

L111   Doulton & Slater's Patent Ware lemonade jug with metal lid; ochre ground, white and pink flowers, with leaves, 1891-1901
Height: 17.7cm; diameter: 20 max.cm
Assistants: Emily J. Partington, Helena M. Pennett ?
Stoneware; impressed, *pâte-sur-pâte*, slip outlines. Doulton & Co., Lambeth.

L112   Doulton & Slater's Patent Ware vase, mottled neck, brown ground with large blue chrysanthemums, 1902-12
Height: 27cm; diameter: 13.5cm
Assistants: Emily J. Partington, unidentified
Stoneware; impressed, tube-tool outlines. Royal Doulton, Lambeth.

L113   Vase, *Art Nouveau* design of leaves, clouds and birds, 1902-22
Height: 18cm; diameter: 13.5cm
Designer unknown.
Hawke's Bay Cultural Trust, Hawke's Bay Museum, Napier. 57/63/6

L114   Slip-cast vase, *Art Nouveau* pattern of yellow and white checks with alternating scroll, 1910-22
Height: 14.8cm; diameter: 15cm
Designer: **Harry Rowe**
Walter C. Cook Decorative Art Collection, Museum of New Zealand Te Papa Tongarewa.

L115   Slip-cast vase, *Art Nouveau* fruit design, green plums, 1910-22
Height: 18.3cm; diameter: 9cm
Designer: **Margaret E. Thompson**
Walter C. Cook Decorative Art Collection, Museum of New Zealand Te Papa Tongarewa.

L116   Slip-cast vase, *Art Nouveau* fruit design, yellow plums and green leaves, 1910-22
Height: 15cm; diameter: 12cm
Designer: **Margaret E. Thompson**
Walter C. Cook Decorative Art Collection, Museum of New Zealand Te Papa Tongarewa.

L117 **Slip-cast vase,** *Art Nouveau* **floral design, vertical arrangements of flowers with three pairs of leaves, 1910-1922**
Height: 20.2cm; diameter: 12cm
Designer: **Margaret E. Thompson**
Walter C. Cook Decorative Art Collection, Museum of New Zealand Te Papa Tongarewa.

L118 **Marqueterie Ware cornucopia vase, blue, fawn and white with gilding, 1891-1906**
Height: 16.9cm; length: 9.9cm; width: 5.7cm
Designer: Unknown
Doulton & Co., Lambeth.
Museum of Applied Arts and Sciences, Sydney, Australia. A3638

L119 **Marqueterie Ware ornamental jug, blue, fawn and white with gilded flowers, 1887-91**
Height: 34.5cm; diameter: 8.9cm
Designer: Unknown
Doulton & Co., Lambeth.

L120 **Marqueterie Ware dish in form of fish, blue, fawn and white with encircling bands and gilded fins and tail, 1887-91**
Height: 9cm; length: 29cm; width: 9cm
Designer: Unknown
Doulton & Co., Lambeth.
Art Gallery of New South Wales Collection. 2543

L121 **Persian Ware vase, pointed leaves and curling sprays of flowers in blue, red and turquoise on white, 1922-36**
Height: 15.5cm; diameter: 13cm
Designers: **Harry Simeon, William Rowe**
Earthenware; biscuit-painted and glazed. Royal Doulton, Lambeth.

L122 **Persian Ware plaque, geometric border and central floral motif in turquoise and blue on white, 1922-36**
Height: 6cm; diameter: 31cm
Designers: **Harry Simeon, William Rowe**
Earthenware; biscuit-painted and glazed. Royal Doulton, Lambeth.

L123 **Framed terracotta panel,** *Rebekah Leaving Her Father's House To Get Married. Gen.24.58. A Time To Get And A Time To Lose,* **1905**
Length: 53cm; height: 28.5cm
Artist: **George Tinworth**
Terracotta; modelled in high-relief. Royal Doulton, Lambeth.
Canterbury Museum Collection. EC1991.488

L124 **Framed terracotta panel,** *Haman Taking Mordecai Through The Streets Of Persia. Let Him That Thinketh He Standeth Take Heed Lest He Fall. A Lesson For Prime Ministers.*
Length: 61.5cm; height: 28cm
Artist: **George Tinworth**
Terracotta; modelled in high-relief. Doulton & Co., Lambeth.
Hawke's Bay Cultural Trust, Hawke's Bay Museum, Napier. NN3/1

L125 **Framed terracotta panel,** *So They Went And Made The Sepulchre Sure Sealing The Stone And Setting A Watch. The Earth With Her Bars Was About Me,* **c. 1882**
Height: 36cm; diameter: 18cm
Artist: **George Tinworth**
Terracotta; modelled in high-relief. Doulton & Co., Lambeth.
Hawke's Bay Cultural Trust, Hawke's Bay Museum, Napier. NN3/3

L126 **Framed terracotta panel,** *And They Were Exceeding Sorrowful And Began Every One Of Them To Say Unto Him Lord is it i. There Were Great Searchings Of Heart,* **c. 1882**
Length: 36.5cm; height: 18.5cm
Artist: **George Tinworth**
Terracotta; modelled in high-relief. Doulton & Co., Lambeth.
Hawke's Bay Cultural Trust, Hawke's Bay Museum, Napier. NN3/2

Burslem Doulton Wares – Lactolian, Hyperion, Pâte-sur-Pâte, *Spanish Ware*

B1 **Lactolian Ware vase with sea horses and** *Art Nouveau-style flowers, 1902-22*
Height: 15.5cm; diameter: 6cm
Bone china. Royal Doulton, Burslem.
Museum of Applied Arts and Sciences, Sydney, Australia. A2778-121

B2 **Hyperion Ware vase with blue crocus flowers, c. 1902-5**
Height: 14.2cm; diameter: 8.2cm
Bone china. Royal Doulton, Burslem.
Museum of Applied Arts and Sciences, Sydney, Australia. 2778-97

B3 **Hyperion Ware vase with tulips in the** *Art Nouveau* **style, 1902-22**
Height: 33cm; diameter: 10cm
Bone china. Royal Doulton, Burslem.

B4 **Vase decorated with irises, 1891-1901**
Height: 26cm; diameter: 9cm
Artist: **Thomas Phillips**
Bone china; *pâte-sur-pâte* on-glaze and gilding. Doulton & Co., Burslem.
Canterbury Museum Collection. C1991.4

B5 **Vase with white roses, 1891-1902**
Height: 41.9cm; diameter: 18cm
Artist: **Thomas Phillips**
Bone china; *pâte-sur-pâte* on-glaze and gilding. Doulton & Co., Burslem.

B6 **Covered goblet,** *Art Nouveau* **stylized tulips, two handles in form of stylized honesty flowers, c. 1900**
Height: 39cm; diameter: 18cm
Modeller: **Charles J. Noke**
Designer/gilder: **Robert Allen**
Bone china; *pâte-sur-pâte* on-glaze and gilding. Doulton & Co., Burslem [special "Amphora" backstamp].

B7 **Vase, Sèvres-blue ground with gilt-outlined poppies, heavily-gilded rim, vellum mounts, 1886-1891**
Height: 24.5cm; diameter: 19cm
Artist: **Walter Slater**
Bone china; *pâte-sur-pâte*, gilding, vellum glaze. Doulton & Co., Burslem.
Museum of Applied Arts and Sciences, Sydney, Australia. A3613

B8 **Vase, green ground with blue water lilies, in imitation of *cloisonné* ware, c. 1900**
Height: 13cm; diameter: 14cm
Porcellanous ware; enamelled decoration and gilding. Doulton & Co., Burslem [impressed DOULTON'S].

B9 **Spanish Ware vase with modelled dragon handle, 1891-1902**
Height: 39.2cm; diameter: 17 max.cm
Earthenware; modelled, painted and gilded. Doulton & Co., Burslem.

B10 **Spanish Ware cabinet plate with briar roses, 1886-1891**
Diameter: 23cm
Artist: **Walter Slater**
Earthenware; painted and gilded. Doulton & Co., Burslem.
Canterbury Museum Collection. EC176.667

B11 **Spanish Ware octagonal vase with poppies, 1889-1891**
Height: 26.5cm; diameter: 13cm
Earthenware; painted and gilded. Doulton & Co., Burslem.

B12 **Spanish Ware vase with Australian wild flowers, 1889-1891**
Height: 37cm; diameter: 19cm
Artist: **Louis Bilton**
Earthenware; painted and gilded. Doulton & Co., Burslem.

Burslem Doulton Wares – Hand-Painted

B13 **Urn, two handles, orchid decoration,1902-12**
Height: 45cm; diameter: 39.4 max.cm
Artist: **David Dewsberry**
Bone china; hand-painted and gilded. Royal Doulton, Burslem.

B14 **Urn, orchid decoration, 1902-19**
Height: 32.5cm; diameter: 22.5cm
Artist: **David Dewsberry**
Bone china; hand-painted and gilded. Royal Doulton, Burslem.

B15a-b **Pair of vases, pink ground, two panels and two reserves with orchid decoration, c. 1913**
Height: 31.5cm; width: 15cm
Artist: **David Dewsberry**
Bone china; hand-painted and gilded. Royal Doulton, Burslem.

B16 **Vase with continuous scene of women and a girl in a garden, playing music and reading, 1911**
Height: 37cm; diameter: 32.4cm
Artist: **Leslie Johnson**
Bone china; hand-painted, gilded. Royal Doulton, Burslem.
Museum of Applied Arts and Sciences, Sydney, Australia. A3551

B17 ***Dante* vase with two panels in the style of an 18th century landscape with figures, 1902-05**
Height: 71cm; diameter: 31cm
Artist: **Leslie Johnson**
Bone china; mounts with vellum glaze, *pâte-sur-pâte*, gilding, hand-painted decoration. Royal Doulton, Burslem.
Museum of Applied Arts and Sciences, Sydney, Australia. A5909-1,2

B18 **Vase on revolving base, with scenes of woman, children and amorini, after George White, 1930**
Height: 65.7cm; diameter: 20cm
Artist: **Leslie Johnson**
Bone china; hand-painted and gilded. Royal Doulton, Burslem.

B19 **Urn-vase with dancing Classical figure, 1886-91**
Height: 32.6cm; diameter: 15.2cm
Artist: **Jack Hewitt**
Earthenware; hand-painted and gilded. Doulton & Co., Burslem.
Museum of Applied Arts and Sciences, Sydney, Australia. A2778-131

B20 **Dessert service or cabinet plate, *Poppies and Daisies*, 1902 (Made for Tiffany's, New York)**
Diameter: 23.6cm
Artist: **Harry Piper**
Bone china; hand-painted and gilded. Royal Doulton, Burslem.

B21 **Dessert service or cabinet plate, *Eglantine*, 1902 (Made for Tiffany's, New York)**
Diameter: 23.6cm
Artist: **Harry Piper**
Bone china; hand-painted and gilded. Royal Doulton, Burslem.

B22 **Vase, roses and mixed flowers, 1929**
Height: 17cm; diameter: 15cm
Artist: **Jack Price**
Bone china; hand-painted. Royal Doulton, Burslem.

B23 **Cabinet plate, bird and flowers, 1895**
Diameter: 22.5cm
Artist: **Walter Slater**
Bone china; hand-painted, gilded. Doulton & Co., Burslem.

B24 **Cabinet plate, peacock design, 1902**
Diameter: 26cm
Designer: **Robert Allen**
Bone china; hand-painted; raised gold decoration. Royal Doulton, Burslem.

B25 **Dessert service plate, floral decoration, 1891-1901**
Diameter: 23cm
Artist: **Samuel Wilson**
Bone china; hand-painted. Doulton & Co., Burslem.

B26 **Covered urn, Chelsea-style floral decoration, modelled handles terminating in bearded face, 1902-22**
Height: 25cm; diameter: 9.5cm
Artist: **Edwin Wood**
Bone china; hand-painted and gilded, modelled. Royal Doulton, Burslem.

B27 **Game plate, *Grouse,* 1892-1901**
Diameter: 23cm
Artist: **Henry Mitchell**
Bone china; hand-painted and gilded. Doulton & Co., Burslem.

B28 **Vase, *Love's Pilotage,* with Venus and Cupid in a shell boat, 1886-91**
Height: 18.6cm; diameter: 15cm
Artist: **George White**
Bone china; hand-painted, gilded strap handles terminating in masks. Doulton & Co., Burslem.
Museum of Applied Arts and Sciences, Sydney, Australia. A3603

B29 **Vase, *The Bathers,* woman and child by pool, 1902-5**
Height: 29.2cm; diameter: 11cm
Artist: **George White**
Bone china; hand-painted and gilded. Royal Doulton, Burslem.
Canterbury Museum Collection. EC178.44

B30 **Covered vase in a Sèvres style, *Captive Cupid,* Venus holding Cupid with ribbons, 1904**
Height: 23.3cm; diameter: 16cm
Artist: **George White**
Bone china; hand-painted, beaded and gilded; curved filigree handles, gilded. Royal Doulton, Burslem.

B31 **Covered urn, *Autumn Festival,* with continuous scene of dancing women and children, 1902-12**
Height: 31.5cm; diameter: 29cm
Artist: **George White**
Bone china; hand-painted and gilded. Royal Doulton, Burslem.

B32 **Wall plate, *Ophelia,* with peacock and floral border, 1903**
Diameter: 22.5cm
Artist: **George White**
Bone china; hand-painted and gilded. Royal Doulton, Burslem.

B33 **Wall plate, *Juliet,* with peacock and floral border, 1903**
Diameter: 22.5cm
Artist: **George White**
Bone china; hand-painted and gilded. Royal Doulton, Burslem.

B34 **Wall plate, *Ellen Terry as Portia in the Guise of a Doctor of Laws*; border of gilt scrolls, classical "masks" and three reserves with scenes from the *Merchant of Venice* – (1) *The Trial Scene* Shylock claims payment of his bond; (2) *The Casket Scene* Bassanio's choice; (3) *The Flight of Jessica and Lorenzo* My daughter! O my ducats!, 1909**
Diameter: 26cm
Artist: **George White**
Bone china; hand-painted and gilded. Royal Doulton, Burslem.

B35 **Plaque of a woman teaching a young child the violin, 1902-12**
Height: 25cm; width: 20.5cm (framed)
Artist: **George White**
Bone china; hand-painted and gilded. Royal Doulton, Burslem.

B36 **Urn-vase with continuous scene of women, girl and cats in drawing room, 1905**
Height: 70cm; diameter: 21cm
Artist: **George Buttle**
Bone china; hand-painted and gilded; D-shaped handles terminating in dolphins' heads, gilded. Royal Doulton, Burslem.

B37 **Vase with continuous scene of two women in a garden, 1905-11**
Height: 81cm; diameter: 25cm
Artist: **George Buttle**
Bone china; hand-painted and gilded. Royal Doulton, Burslem.

B38 **Vase on revolving base, with continuous scene of a boy and cattle in a rural landscape, 1902-17**
Height: 69cm; diameter: 20cm
Artist: **Charles Beresford Hopkins**
Bone china; hand-painted and gilded; D-shaped handles terminating in dolphins' heads, gilded. Royal Doulton, Burslem.

B39 **Vase, *Bab Souika – Arab Tunis;* continuous scene, 1911**
Height: 42.5cm; diameter: 30cm
Artist: **Harry Allen**
Bone china; hand-painted, gilded scrolls and beading. Royal Doulton, Burslem.

B40 **Vase, *Kairouan;* continuous scene, 1910-22**
Height: 29.5cm; diameter: 15cm
Artist: **Harry Allen**
Bone china; hand-painted, gilded scrolls and beading; elaborate entwined handles, gilded. Royal Doulton, Burslem.

B41 **Dish with scene and four reserves of young missel thrushes, elaborate gilded scrolls and rim, 1914**
Height: 4cm; width: 21.5cm; length: 27.5cm
Artist: **Harry Allen**
Bone china; hand-painted, gilded. Royal Doulton, Burslem.

B42 **Covered urn with gilded filigree foliage and panel with spray of Chelsea-style flowers, 1909-22**
Height: 15cm diameter: 12.6cm
Artist: **Percy Curnock**
Bone china; hand-painted and gilded. Royal Doulton, Burslem.
Museum of Applied Arts and Sciences, Sydney, Australia. A3821-1,2

B43a-b **Tea cup and saucer, pink roses and gilt, 1909**
Cup: Height: 5cm; diameter: 7.8cm. Saucer: diameter: 12cm
Artist: **Percy Curnock**
Bone china; hand-painted and gilded. Royal Doulton, Burslem.

B44 **Biscuit barrel with silver cover and handle, blue and white roses, 1891**
Height: 15.5cm; diameter: 17cm
Artist: **Percy Curnock**
Bone china; hand-painted. Doulton & Co., Burslem.

B45 **Bowl with feather decoration, 1902 -22**
Height: 5.2cm; diameter: 10.5cm
Artist: **Joseph Birbeck Snr**
Earthenware; hand-painted. Royal Doulton, Burslem.

B46 **Vase with owl, poppies and moon, 1891-1901**
Height: 21cm; diameter: 10cm
Artist: **A. Elsin**
Earthenware; low-relief painting, gilded outlines. Doulton & Co., Burslem.

B47 **Vase, *Mount Cook and Hookers Glacier,* 1891-1901**
Height: 18cm; diameter: 17cm
Artist: **Leonard Bentley**
Bone china; hand-painted. Doulton & Co., Burslem.

B48 **Vase with foliage, heraldic motifs and motto, *Nought is more honourable to a Knight, than to defend the feeble in their Right,* 1919**
Height: 32cm; diameter: 26.3cm
Artist: **Reco Capey**
Porcellanous ware; painted and stencilled. Royal Doulton, Burslem. (Erroneously marked with a Flambé backstamp.)

B49 **Covered urn vase, two panels depicting Venus and amorini, c. 1892**
Height: 42.5cm; width: 24cm
Artist: **Charles Labarre**
Bone china; hand-painted with modelled and vellum glazed mounts (probably by Charles Noke). Doulton & Co., Burslem.

B50 **Vase, *Whoa Steady,* 1930s**
Height: 42cm; diameter: 15.5cm
Artist: **Rowland Holdcroft**
Bone china: hand-painted. Royal Doulton, Burslem.

B51 **Vase, *Lady Hamilton after Joshua Reynolds R.A.,* 1891-1901**
Height: 21.5cm; diameter: 16.5cm
Artist: **Fred Sutton**
Bone china: hand-painted. Doulton & Co., Burslem.

B52 **Vase, sprays of roses; pedestal base with raised gilding and modelling, 1902-5**
Height: 66cm; diameter: 21.5cm
Artist: **Edward Raby**
Bone china; hand-painted and gilded; raised *pâte-sur-pâte* and gilded decoration on foot. Royal Doulton, Burslem.

B53 **Covered urn-vase with handles, sprays of pink and cream roses, 1912**
Height: 31.8cm; diameter: 11.2cm
Artist: **Edward Raby**
Bone china; hand-painted and gilded. Royal Doulton, Burslem.
Museum of Applied Arts and Sciences, Sydney, Australia. A5183-1,2

B54 **Vase, *Fair in My Garden Buds the Rose*; sprays of pink roses on a mauve ground, 1902-19**
Height: 50.7cm; diameter: 15.2cm
Artist: **Edward Raby**
Bone china; hand-painted; gilded rim and foot. Royal Doulton, Burslem.

B55 **Vase, sprays of sweet peas, 1902-19**
Height: 49.5cm; diameter: 24.4 max.cm
Artist: **Edward Raby**
Bone china; hand-painted; gilded rim and foot. Royal Doulton, Burslem.
Art Gallery of New South Wales Collection. 2024

B56 **Luscian Ware vase, poppies, 1898-1901**
Height: 28cm; diameter: 8.8cm
Artist: **Edward Raby**
Bone china; hand-painted. Doulton & Co., Burslem. (Special Luscian Ware backstamp).
Art Gallery of New South Wales Collection. 2023

B57a-b **Pair of vases, landscapes with roses and fountain, painted in the Cadbury Gardens, England, 1913**
Height: 18cm; diameter: 11cm
Artist: **Edward Raby**
Bone china; hand-painted; gilded rim and foot. Royal Doulton, Burslem.

B58 **Vase, delphiniums, 1902-19**
Height: 24.5cm; diameter: 14cm
Artist: **Edward Raby**
Bone china; hand-painted; gilded rim. Royal Doulton, Burslem.

B59 **Vase, white roses in the moonlight, 1902-19**
Height: 31cm; diameter: 17cm
Artist: **Edward Raby**
Bone china; hand-painted; pale pink glaze inner rim; gilded rim and foot. Royal Doulton, Burslem.

B60 **Hexagonal ginger jar, pink wisteria and a pair of birds, 1902-19**
Height: 20cm; diameter: 14.5cm
Artist: **Edward Raby**
Bone china; hand-painted, gilded. Royal Doulton, Burslem.

B61 **Vase, procession of Japanese women through grove of trees with lanterns, 1902-19**
Height: 24.2cm; diameter: 10cm
This piece is unsigned but the Doulton factory label reads: "By Raby. £6-10-0"
Bone china; hand-painted. Royal Doulton, Burslem.
Art Gallery of New South Wales Collection. 2038

B62 **Covered urn on plinth, irises, 1892-1901**
Height: 30cm; diameter: 14cm
Artist: **Louis Bilton**
Bone china; hand-painted, with *pâte-sur-pâte* and gilding. Doulton & Co., Burslem.
Art Gallery of New South Wales Collection. 2040

B63 **Ewer-vase, modelled handle terminating in ram's head, low-relief gilded birds, flowers and foliage; embossed gilded collar; four painted panels of waratahs separated by putti and swags, c. 1892**
Height: 68cm; diameter: 17 max.cm
Artist: **Louis Bilton**
Modelling possibly by Charles Noke; gilding design possibly by Robert Allen.
Bone china; hand-painted, modelled and gilded. Doulton & Co., Burslem.
Museum of Applied Arts and Sciences, Sydney, Australia. A3826

B64 **Vase, *The Monastery Door*, 1902-22**
Height: 41.7cm; diameter: 20.2cm
Artist: **Harry Tittensor**
Bone china; hand-painted. Royal Doulton, Burslem.

B65 **Vase, *The Knight Errant*, 1902-22**
Height: 44cm
Artist: **Harry Tittensor**
Bone china; hand-painted. Royal Doulton, Burslem.

B66 **Vase on plinth, elegant couple in a garden, 1902-22**
Height: 110cm
Artist: **Harry Tittensor**
Bone china; hand-painted. Royal Doulton, Burslem.
Museum of New Zealand Te Papa Tongarewa Collection.

B67 **Dish, *The Gulf of Venice*, 1915**
Length: 26.5cm; width: 20cm
Artist: **John Hugh Plant**
Bone china; hand-painted, gilded. Royal Doulton, Burslem.
Canterbury Museum Collection. C1991.2

B68 **Dish, *The Salute Canal, Venice*, 1915**
Length: 26.5cm; width: 20cm
Artist: **John Hugh Plant**
Bone china; hand-painted, gilded. Royal Doulton, Burslem.

B69 **Plate, *St Marks, Venice*, 1916**
Diameter: 20.5cm
Artist: **John Hugh Plant**
Bone china; hand-painted, gilded. Royal Doulton, Burslem.

B70 **Plate, *San Geremia, Venice*, 1916**
Diameter: 20.5cm
Artist: **John Hugh Plant**
Bone china; hand-painted, gilded. Royal Doulton, Burslem.

B71 **Enamelled panel, *Vanity, Juno's Bird*, c. 1900**
Height: 17.8cm; length: 29.5cm
Artists: **Charles J. Noke and William G. Hodkinson**
Art Gallery of New South Wales Collection. 11230

B72 **Enamelled panel, untitled (woman with cherub), 1898**
Height: 8.7cm; length: 19.3cm
Artists: **Charles J. Noke and William G. Hodkinson**
Art Gallery of New South Wales Collection. 7155

B73 **Enamelled panel, *Dolce Far Niente*, c. 1900**
Height: 18.4cm; width: 18.4cm
Artists: **Charles J. Noke and William G. Hodkinson**
Art Gallery of New South Wales Collection. 1227

B74 **Enamelled panel with ceramic frame, untitled (Pan and two women), c. 1900**
Height: 21.5cm; length: 39.5cm
Artists: **Charles J. Noke and William G. Hodkinson**
Museum of Applied Arts and Sciences, Sydney, Australia. A3575

B75 **Enamelled panel, *Isabella and the Pot of Basil*, c. 1900.**
Height: 31.7cm; width: 23.2cm

Burslem Doulton Wares – Special Glazes

B76 **Wall Plaque, *Mermaids*, 1891-1901**
Diameter: 31cm
Designer: **John Slater**
Earthenware; lustre glazed and gilded. Doulton & Co., Burslem.
Museum of Applied Arts and Sciences, Sydney, Australia. A2778.337

B77 **Experimental jug, low-relief portrait based on Rembrandt's *Man in Armour*, 1890s**
Height: 19cm; diameter: 15cm
Artist: **Charles Noke**
Coarse marl earthenware; painted slip; lead and iron glaze. Doulton & Co., Burslem.
Museum of Applied Arts and Sciences, Sydney, Australia. A3803

B78 **Rembrandt Ware jardinière, *Sancho Panza "Asked if the dinner was only to show off sleight of hand"*, 1902-10**
Height: 30.4cm; diameter: 32.1cm
Artist: **Walter Nunn**
Coarse marl earthenware; painted slip. Royal Doulton, Burslem.
Museum of Applied Arts and Sciences, Sydney, Australia. A4605

B79 **Rembrandt Ware covered vase with *Self Portrait* after Rembrandt – *A Contented Mind Is A Blessing Kind*, 1898-1901**
Height: 38cm; diameter: 23cm
Artist: **Arthur Eaton**
Coarse marl earthenware; painted slip; copper cover. Royal Doulton, Burslem.
Museum of Applied Arts and Sciences, Sydney, Australia. A939-1,2

B80 **Rembrandt Ware vase, *King Charles I* (after Van Dyck), 1902-10**
Height: 42.6cm; diameter: 16.5cm
Artist: **Walter Nunn**
Coarse marl earthenware; painted slip. Royal Doulton, Burslem.
Museum of Applied Arts and Sciences, Sydney, Australia. A5912

B81 **Holbein Ware vase, *King Charles I* (after Van Dyck), 1902-10**
Height: 29.3cm; diameter: 8.5cm
Artist: **Walter Nunn**
Porcellaneous ware; painted slip. Royal Doulton, Burslem.
Canterbury Museum Collection. EC143.73

B82 **Rembrandt Ware vase, windmills in winter landscape,** *Doth My Simple Feature Yet Content You,* **1902-10**
Height: 33cm; diameter: 18cm
Artist: **Walter Nunn**
Coarse marl earthenware; painted slip. Royal Doulton, Burslem.
Canterbury Museum Collection. EC178.54

B83 **Holbein Ware jardinière, tavern scene with a Royalist tippler and two Puritans, 1902-10**
Height: 34cm; diameter: 40.5cm
Artist: **Walter Nunn**
Porcellaneous ware; painted slip. Royal Doulton, Burslem.

B84 **Holbein Ware vase, man in "Elizabethan" costume, 1902-15**
Height: 18.5cm; diameter: 7.2cm
Artist: **Harry Tittensor**
Porcellaneous ware; painted slip. Royal Doulton, Burslem.
Museum of Applied Arts and Sciences, Sydney, Australia. A2778-170

B85 **Rembrandt Ware covered vase, portrait of ? Cromwell,** *With A Conscience Clear We Need Not Fear,* **1898-1915**
Height: 45.7cm; diameter: 23.8cm
Artist: **Arthur Eaton**
Coarse marl earthenware; painted slip; copper cover and foot. Doulton, Burslem.
Canterbury Museum Collection. C1973.27

B86 **Rembrandt Ware jardinière, portrait of an old judge,** *Corruption Wins Not More Than Honesty,* **1902-15**
Height: 27.5cm; diameter: 34cm
Artist: **Harry Tittensor**
Coarse marl earthenware; painted slip. Royal Doulton, Burslem.

B87 **Kingsware flagon with stopper,** *Pied Piper*
B88 **Kingsware flagon with metal stopper,** *The Pipe Major*
B89 **Kingsware vase with handles,** *Falstaff*
B90 **Kingsware vase with handles,** *Here's a Health unto His Majesty*
B91 **Kingsware figural flask,** *Watchman*
B92 **Kingsware flagon,** *George the Guard*
B93 **Kingsware small vase with handles,** *The Lynton Witch*
B94 **Kingsware flagon with metal stopper,** *The Jovial Monk*
B95 **Kingsware flagon with metal stopper,** *Oyez! Oyez!*
B96 **Kingsware flagon,** *Stiggins*
B97 **Kingsware flagon with silver stopper,** *Hooked*
B98 **Kingsware teapot,** *Don Quixote and Sancho Panza*
B99 **Kingsware flagon,** *Bonnie Prince Charlie*
B100 **Kingsware flagon,** *Micawber – the Ever-Expectant*
B101 **Kingsware flask,** *Wizard*
B102 **Kingsware flagon,** *Sporting Squire*
B103 **Kingsware flagon with metal stopper,** *Nelson*
B104 **Kingsware flagon,** *Golfers*
B105 **Embossed Ware flagon with metal stopper,** *Uncle Sam*
B106 **Embossed Ware flagon,** *Tony Weller*
B107 **Queens Ware flagon,** *Monk*
B108 **Queens Ware flagon,** *Micawber*
All earthenwares; slip-cast. Royal Doulton, Burslem.

B109 **Mottled Flambé vase, 1904-5**
Height: 29cm; diameter: 8cm
Earthenware; transmutation glaze. Royal Doulton, Burslem.
Canterbury Museum Collection. EC141.249

B110 **Flambé vase with enamelled and gilded Chinese dragon, 1904-5**
Height: 22.8cm; diameter: 9.3cm
Earthenware; transmutation glaze. Royal Doulton, Burslem.
Canterbury Museum Collection. EC141.256

B111 **Rouge Flambé vase with gilded carp and water lilies, 1904-6**
Height: 52cm; diameter: 16cm
Artist: **William G. Hodkinson**
Earthenware; transmutation glaze. Royal Doulton, Burslem.

B112 **Gold Flambé double gourd vase, 1904-6**
Height: 13.5cm; diameter: 7.5 max.cm
Earthenware; transmutation glaze. Royal Doulton, Burslem.
Art Gallery of New South Wales Collection. 2026

B113 **Rouge Flambé vase with gilded and enamelled carp and water lilies, 1904-12**
Height: 21cm; diameter: 36cm
Artist: **William G. Hodkinson**
Earthenware; transmutation glaze. Royal Doulton, Burslem.

B114 **Mottled Flambé onion vase, 1904-23**
Height: 16.5cm; diameter: 8.5cm
Signed : **Noke**
Earthenware; transmutation glaze. Impressed DOULTON'S. Royal Doulton, Burslem.

B115 **Flambé triple gourd vase, 1904-23**
Height: 18.5cm; diameter: 9 max.cm
Earthenware; transmutation glaze. Royal Doulton, Burslem.

B116 **Flambé vase with gilded eagle, 1904-20**
Height: 20cm; diameter: 17cm
Signed : **Harry Nixon**
Earthenware; transmutation glaze. Royal Doulton, Burslem.
Hawke's Bay Cultural Trust, Hawke's Bay Museum, Napier. 57/63/5

B117 **Flambé jardinière with enamelled and gilded Viking ship, 1904-20**
Height: 42cm; diameter: 43cm
Original price label £38/10/-.
Earthenware; transmutation glaze. Royal Doulton, Burslem.

B118 **Flambé vase with stencilled design of mermaids and fish, 1920s**
Height: 18.4cm; diameter: 17.7cm
Earthenware; transmutation glaze. Royal Doulton, Burslem.
Canterbury Museum Collection. EC178.45

B119 Flambé vase with under-glaze print of a country cottage and garden, 1910-20s
Height: 27.5cm; diameter: 23.5cm
Earthenware; transmutation glaze. Royal Doulton, Burslem.

B120 Flambé vase with under-glaze illustration of gnomes, 1915-22
Height: 28cm; diameter: 25cm
Original price label £52/10/-.
Earthenware; transmutation glaze. Royal Doulton, Burslem.
Art Gallery of New South Wales Collection. 2034

B121 Flambé vase with under-glaze painting of foliage, 1915-20s
Height: 19cm; diameter: 8 max.cm
Earthenware; transmutation glaze. Royal Doulton, Burslem.
Art Gallery of New South Wales Collection. 2026

B122 Flambé vase with modelled Egyptian heads and under-glaze print of Arab desert scene, 1923-7
Height: 30cm; diameter: 10.7 max.cm
Earthenware; transmutation glaze. Royal Doulton, Burslem.

B123 Flambé pomegranate vase, c. 1945-50
Height: 17.3cm; diameter: 15.8cm
Signed : **Charles J. Noke [sic] and Fred Moore**
Earthenware; transmutation glaze. Royal Doulton, Burslem.
Hawke's Bay Cultural Trust, Hawke's Bay Museum, Napier. 86/116/1

B124 *Rouge et Noir* Flambé vase, June – October 1953-4
Height: 22.7cm; diameter: 20cm
Earthenware; transmutation glaze. Royal Doulton, Burslem.

B125 Sung jardinière with peacock and iridescent effects, 1920-28
Height: 27.2cm; length: 43cm; width: 24.5cm
Signed: **Charles J. Noke**
Earthenware; transmutation glaze. Royal Doulton, Burslem.

B126 Sung vase, *The Alchemist*, 1920-25
Height: 46cm; diameter: 23cm
Signed: **Charles J. Noke**
Earthenware; transmutation glaze. Royal Doulton, Burslem.

B127 Sung bowl with peacock, 1920-30s
Height: 9.5cm; diameter: 37cm
Earthenware; transmutation glaze. Royal Doulton, Burslem.

B128 Veined Sung vase, under-glaze decoration of prunus blossom, 1947
Height: 33cm; diameter: 32cm
Signed: **Charles J. Noke [sic] and Fred Moore**
Earthenware; transmutation glaze. Royal Doulton, Burslem.

B129 Sung vase with under-glaze painting of stag and deer in the Highlands, *The King of the Glen*, 1930s
Height: 41.3cm; diameter: 23cm
Signed : **Noke and (Harry) Nixon**
Earthenware; transmutation glaze. Royal Doulton, Burslem.

B130 Sung pomegranate jardinière, floral under-glaze decoration, 1932-40
Height: 60.5cm; diameter: 53cm
Signed : **Noke and (Harry) Nixon**
Earthenware; transmutation glaze over hand-painted decoration, on-glaze enamelling and gilding. Royal Doulton, Burslem.
Museum of Applied Arts and Sciences, Sydney, Australia. A5911

B131 Sung vase with mottled effects, 1947
Height: 33cm; diameter: 32cm
Signed: **Charles J.Noke [sic] and Fred Moore**
Earthenware; transmutation glaze. Royal Doulton, Burslem.
Walter C. Cook Decorative Art Collection, Museum of New Zealand Te Papa Tongarewa.

B132 Veined Sung with prunus blossom decoration, c. 1933
Height: 24cm; diameter: 13cm
Signed: **Noke**
Earthenware; transmutation glaze. Royal Doulton, Burslem.

B133 Sung covered ginger jar with mottled effects, 1933-40s
Height: 13cm; diameter: 12cm
Signed: **Fred Allen**
Earthenware; transmutation glaze. Royal Doulton, Burslem.
Hawke's Bay Cultural Trust, Hawke's Bay Museum, Napier. 57/63/4

B134 Sung vase with fish and seaweed, 1928-40
Height: 13.5cm; diameter: 9cm
Signed: **Noke and Fred Allen**
Earthenware; transmutation glaze. Royal Doulton, Burslem.
Hawke's Bay Cultural Trust, Hawke's Bay Museum, Napier. 57/63/3

B135 Crystalline vase, yellow glaze, 1904-18
Height: 16.9cm; diameter: 17.5 max.cm
Porcellanous ware; zinc oxide glaze. Royal Doulton, Burslem.
Otago Museum, Dunedin. F49.221

B136 Crystalline vase, white glaze, 1904-5
Height: 21.5cm; diameter: 20 max.cm
Porcellanous ware; zinc oxide glaze. Royal Doulton, Burslem.
Otago Museum, Dunedin. F49.220

B137 Crystalline double-gourd vase, white glaze, 1904-5
Porcellanous ware; zinc oxide glaze. Royal Doulton, Burslem.

B138 **Crystalline vase, celadon green and teal blue glaze, 1904-18**
Height: 21.1cm; diameter: 7cm
Porcellanous ware; zinc oxide glaze. Royal Doulton, Burslem.
Museum of Applied Arts and Sciences, Sydney, Australia. A2741

B139 **Crystalline vase, blue glaze and beaten metal lid with ceramic button, 1904-5**
Height: 6.5cm; diameter: 10.8cm
Porcellanous ware; zinc oxide glaze. Royal Doulton, Burslem.

B140 **Crystalline onion vase, white glaze, 1904-5**
Height: 27.8cm; diameter: 9 max.cm
Porcellanous ware; zinc oxide glaze. Royal Doulton, Burslem. (Special "Amphora" backstamp, impressed DOULTON'S.)

B141 **Titanian bowl with oil-spot effects on blue-green ground, 1915-25**
Diameter: 35.5cm
Bone china; titanium glaze. Royal Doulton, Burslem.

B142 **Titanian vase, Persian-style flowers on a blue-grey ground, 1921**
Height: 17.2cm
Bone china; titanium glaze, gilding. Royal Doulton, Burslem.
Walter C. Cook Decorative Art Collection, Museum of New Zealand Te Papa Tongarewa.

B143 **Titanian vase, hand-painted peacock on a branch with blossoms, blue ground, 1915-19**
Height: 34.5cm; diameter: 15cm
Artist: **Edward Raby**
Bone china; titanium glaze. Royal Doulton, Burslem.

B144 **Titanian hexagonal vase, decorated in the Japanese manner with peacocks and flowers, on a variegated blue ground, 1915-25**
Height: 19.1cm; diameter: 8.6cm
Bone china; titanium glaze, gilding. Royal Doulton, Burslem.
Otago Museum, Dunedin. F45.94

B145 **Titanian vase with dragonflies and roses, blue ground, 1915-25**
Height: 24cm
Bone china; titanium glaze, gilding. Royal Doulton, Burslem.

B146 **Titanian figurine of a goblin-like creature with webbed feet, wearing a "Union Jack" vest, smoking a pipe and holding a goblet, 1915-25**
Height: 10.2cm; diameter: 10cm
Bone china; slip-cast; titanium glaze. Royal Doulton, Burslem.

B147 **Titanian bowl, *Wood Boy and Rabbits*, on a green ground, 1915-25**
Height: 5.3cm; diameter: 15.5cm
Artist: **Harry Tittensor**
Bone china; titanium glaze, hand-painted. Royal Doulton, Burslem.
Art Gallery of New South Wales Collection. 2044

B148 **Titanian jug-vase, *Out in the Cold, Pierrot Disconsolate*, on a pale blue ground, 1915-25**
Height: 23.5cm; length: 11.5cm; width: 8.2cm
Original price label £10/10/6
Artist: **Harry Tittensor**
Bone china; titanium glaze, hand-painted. Royal Doulton, Burslem.
Mrs Noeline Bain.

B149 **Titanian vase, scene from *The Rubaiyat of Omar Khayyam*, 1918**
Inscription on base is Quatrain 37 from the *Rubaiyat*:
Ah fill the cup:- What boots it to repeat
How the time is slipping underneath our feet
Unborn tomorrow and dead yesterday
Why fret about them if today be sweet
Height: 43.5cm; diameter: 21cm
Artist: **Harry Tittensor**
Bone china; titanium glaze, hand-painted. Royal Doulton, Burslem.

B150 **Titanian vase, scene from *The Rubaiyat of Omar Khayyam*, c. 1918**
Inscription on base (now illegible) is Quatrain 36 from the *Rubaiyat*: *The Potter's Shop*.
Height: 44.3cm; diameter: 23cm
Artist: **Harry Tittensor**
Bone china; titanium glaze, hand-painted. Royal Doulton, Burslem.
Dunedin Public Art Gallery Collection.

B151a-b **Titanian coffee cup and saucer, peacock motif on a blue-green ground, 1915-25**
Bone china; titanium glaze, hand-painted. Royal Doulton, Burslem.

B152 **Titanian vase, white cat on a branch, with blossom spray on a blue ground, 1915-23**
Height: 17cm; diameter: 15cm
Artist: **Harry Allen**
Bone china; titanium glaze, hand-painted. Royal Doulton, Burslem.

B6153 **Titanian (?) vase, owl on a pine tree branch, dark blue ground, 1915-23**
Height: 24.7cm; diameter: 8.3cm
Artist: **Harry Allen**
Bone china; titanium (?) glaze, hand-painted. Royal Doulton, Burslem.

B154 **Titanian vase, baby bird on a blossoming branch, blue ground, 1915-23**
Height: 9.5cm; diameter: 6cm
Unsigned.
Bone china; titanium glaze, hand-painted. Royal Doulton, Burslem.

B155 **Titanian vase, heron on a pale lavender ground, 1915-1923**
Height: 7.5cm; diameter: 5cm
Artist: **Harry Allen**
Bone china; titanium glaze, hand-painted. Royal Doulton, Burslem.

B156 **Titanian vase, *Young Missel Thrush*, on a blue ground**
Height: 14.5cm; diameter: 7.5cm
Artist: **F. Henri**
Bone china; titanium glaze, hand-painted. Royal Doulton, Burslem.

B157 **Titanian vase,*Young Warblers,* on a blue ground, 1919**
Height: 18cm; diameter: 15cm
Artist: **Harry Allen**
Bone china; titanium glaze, hand-painted. Royal Doulton,
Burslem.

B158 **Titanian bowl, polar bear and cub on ice floes, blue-green ground, 1915-23**
Height: 5.32cm; diameter: 15.8cm
Artist: **Harry Allen**
Bone china; titanium glaze, hand-painted. Royal Doulton,
Burslem.
Canterbury Museum Collection. C1991.3

B159 **Titanian vase, *Lords of the North* – polar bears in sea, with sea gulls; blue ground. Impressed date 1919, backstamp 1923-5**
Height: 39cm; diameter: 18cm
Artist: **Harry Allen**
Bone china; titanium glaze, hand-painted. Royal Doulton,
Burslem.

B160 **Lustre and Titanian figurine group of two embracing monkeys, 1920**
Height: 6.8cm; length: 8.3cm; width: 5.7cm
Bone china; slip-cast, lustre and titanium glazes. Royal
Doulton, Burslem.
*Museum of Applied Arts and Sciences, Sydney, Australia.
A3634*

B161 **Lustre vase with floral decoration, 1912**
Height: 17cm; diameter: 5.5cm
Earthenware; lustre glaze. Royal Doulton, Burslem.

B162 **Chinese Jade vase with low-relief foliage, 1930**
Height: 14.7cm; diameter: 7.5cm
Signed : **Noke [sic]**
Earthenware; modelled and glazed. Royal Doulton,
Burslem.
*Museum of Applied Arts and Sciences, Sydney, Australia.
A2771*

B163 **Chinese Jade lamp base with low-relief foliage, 1920-1940s**
Height: 26cm; diameter: 20.5cm [not including light fitting]
Signed : **Noke [sic]**
Earthenware; modelled and glazed. Royal Doulton,
Burslem.

B164 **Vase with plain yellow glaze and fretted wooden Chinese cover, 1930s**
Height: 34.5cm; diameter: 23.5cm [including cover]
Bone china. Royal Doulton, Burslem.

B165 **Chang goblet vase on a decorated Sung base, 1925-30s**
Signed: **Noke and (Harry) Nixon**
Earthenware; transmutation glazes. Royal Doulton,
Burslem.

B166 **Chang globular vase, 1925-30s**
Height: 14cm; diameter: 14cm
Signed: **Noke and (Harry) Nixon**
Earthenware; transmutation glazes. Royal Doulton,
Burslem.
*Hawke's Bay Cultural Trust, Hawke's Bay Museum, Napier.
57/63/7*

B167 **Chang tapered cylinder vase with sloping shoulder, 1925-30s**
Height: 17cm; diameter: 9.2cm
Signed: **Noke and (Harry) Nixon**
Earthenware; transmutation glazes. Royal Doulton,
Burslem.

B168 **Chang goblet, 1925-30s**
Height: 10.5cm; diameter: 12cm
Signed: **Noke and (Harry) Nixon**
Earthenware; transmutation glazes. Royal Doulton,
Burslem.

B169 **Chang bowl, 1925-30s**
Height: 4.3cm; diameter: 8.7cm
Signed: **Noke and (Harry) Nixon**
Earthenware; transmutation glazes. Royal Doulton,
Burslem.

B170 **Chang bottle with sloping shoulders, 1925-30s**
Height: 22.4cm; diameter: 7cm
Signed: **Noke and (Harry) Nixon**
Earthenware; transmutation glazes. Royal Doulton,
Burslem.

B171 **Chang globular vase, 1925-30s**
Height: 17.5cm; diameter: 17cm
Signed: **Noke and (Harry) Nixon**
Earthenware; transmutation glazes. Royal Doulton,
Burslem.

B172 **Chang rectangular "Chinese" vase with handles, 1925-1930s**
Height: 32cm; length: 21cm; width: 25cm
Signed: **Noke and (Harry) Nixon**
Earthenware; transmutation glazes. Royal Doulton,
Burslem.
*Museum of New Zealand Te Papa Tongarewa Collection.
C386*

B173 **Chang vase with modelled dragon, 1930-40**
Height: 20.5cm; diameter: 20cm
Artist: **Charles Noke**
Earthenware; transmutation glazes. Royal Doulton,
Burslem.

B174 **Chang lamp, *The Potter*, 1933-4**
Height: 30cm; diameter: 17cm
Artist: **Charles Noke**
Earthenware; transmutation glazes. Royal Doulton,
Burslem.

B175 **Chang "mutton fat" plaque, 1925-30s**
Diameter: 31cm
Signed: **Noke**
Earthenware; transmutation glazes. Royal Doulton,
Burslem.

Lambeth Doulton Commemorative Wares

L127   **Jug issued to commemorate H. M. Stanley and the Emin Pasha Relief Expedition of 1887-9.** *Out of Darkness Into Light,* **1890**
Height: 19.4cm; diameter: 18.5cm
Salt-glazed stoneware; top dipped in darker glaze; low-relief modelling. Doulton & Co., Lambeth.

L128   **Commemorative jug issued for the coronation of King Edward VII and Queen Alexandra, 1902**
Stoneware; low-relief modelling. Royal Doulton, Lambeth.

Burslem Doulton Commemorative Wares

B176   **Commemorative beaker issued for the Golden Jubilee of Queen Victoria, with portraits of the Queen, laurel leaves, and inscription** *J. T. Bourne from Sir Henry Doulton,* **1887**
Bone china; monochrome transfer print, gilding. Doulton & Co., Burslem.
The late Herbert Mawdesley Bourne.

B177   **Commemorative tyg for Queen Victoria's Diamond Jubilee, showing the Queen's portrait, a crown and the Royal Standard; handles in the form of dragons, 1897**
Height: 16.8cm; diameter: 11.2 max.cm
Bone china; polychrome transfer prints, modelling and gilding. Doulton, Burslem.
Museum of Applied Arts and Sciences, Sydney, Australia. A3630

B178   **Luscian Ware vase with portrait of a beefeater;** *God Bless Her.* **(Queen Victoria's Diamond Jubilee), 1897**
Height: 28cm; diameter: 12cm
Artist: **Walter Nunn**
Bone china; hand-painted. Doulton & Co., Burslem.

B179   **Jug issued to commemorate the death of the Right Honourable William Ewart Gladstone, British Liberal politician and Prime Minister; portrait of Gladstone and replica of his coat-of-arms, 1898**
Parian with vellum glaze, low-relief modelling. Doulton & Co., Burslem.

B180   **Coffee cup and saucer from a service made for the Officers' Saloon on the** *Discovery,* **for Robert Falcon Scott's British Antarctic Expedition of 1901-4. Crest with a penguin and icebergs within a garter, 1900**
Bone china; transfer print and gilding. Doulton & Co., Burslem.
Canterbury Museum Collection. A180.4

B181   **Coffee cup and saucer with picture and crest of Banks Peninsula sailing vessel,** *M. Y. Taranui,* **c. 1928**
Bone china; transfer print. Royal Doulton, Burslem.

B182   **Limited Edition loving cup issued for the Silver Jubilee of King George V and Queen Mary. Number 957 of edition of 1000, 1935**
Height: 25.5cm; width: 24cm
Designers: **Charles Noke and Harry Fenton**
Earthenware; low-relief modelling. Royal Doulton, Burslem.

B183   **Limited Edition loving cup issued for the coronation of Edward VIII. Number 684 of edition of 2000, 1937**
Height: 26cm; width: 27.4cm
Designers: **Charles Noke and Harry Fenton**
Earthenware; low-relief modelling. Royal Doulton, Burslem.

B184   **Limited edition loving cup issued to commemorate the coronation of Queen Elizabeth II. Number 557 of edition of 1000, 1953**
Height: 26.7cm; diameter: 27cm
Designer: **Cecil J. Noke**
Earthenware; low-relief modelling, photographic transfer prints. Royal Doulton, Burslem.
Canterbury Museum Collection. EC178.56

Lambeth Doulton New Zealand Wares

L129   **Maori Ware spill vase, 1905-23**
Height: 27.5cm; diameter (base): 13.5cm
Salt-glazed stoneware; applied medallions and darker glaze bands. Royal Doulton, Lambeth.

L130   **Maori Ware teapot, c. 1906-20**
Height: 14.4cm; diameter: 12.4cm
Salt-glazed stoneware; applied medallions and darker glaze bands. Royal Doulton, Lambeth.
Auckland Museum Collection. K5135

L131   **Maori Ware bowl, c. 1906-20**
Height: 6.7cm; diameter: 13cm
Salt-glazed stoneware; applied medallions and darker glaze bands. Royal Doulton, Lambeth.
Auckland Museum Collection. C6675

L132   **Maori Ware flagon with stopper, c. 1906-20**
Height: 6.7cm; diameter: 13cm
Salt-glazed stoneware; applied medallions and darker glaze bands. Royal Doulton, Lambeth.
Auckland Museum Collection. K5475.1/2

L133   **Maori Ware vase, c. 1906-20**
Height: 15.8cm; diameter: 7.5cm
Salt-glazed stoneware; applied medallions and darker glaze bands. Royal Doulton, Lambeth.
Auckland Museum Collection. K5495

L134   **Kia Ora (Maori) Ware jug, 1920s**
Height: 12.2cm; diameter: 17.8cm
Salt-glazed stoneware; applied medallions. Royal Doulton, Lambeth.

Burslem Doulton New Zealand Wares

B185a-c **Commemorative cup, saucer and plate issued for the Canterbury Jubilee Exhibition.** The transfer prints illustrate the exhibition buildings, John Robert Godley, the so-called Founder of Canterbury (the Canterbury Association Agent), and William Reece, Mayor of Christchurch, **1900**
Cup: Height: 7.5cm; width: 8.5cm
Saucer: Diameter: 15.5cm
Plate: Diameter: 19cm
Earthenware; sepia transfer prints, gilding. Doulton & Co., Burslem.
Canterbury Museum Collection. EC158.237-8

B186 **Commemorative "horseshoe" teapot stand, issued for the Canterbury Jubilee Exhibition.** The transfer prints illustrate Christchurch Anglican Cathedral, and John Robert Godley, **1900**
Height: 2.3cm; length: 19.5cm; width: 15.3cm
Earthenware; sepia transfer prints, gilding. Doulton & Co., Burslem.

B187 **Teapot issued to commemorate Richard John Seddon, Premier of New Zealand,** *He stood for Empire,* **1906**
Height: 11.5cm; length: 17cm; width: 9.5cm
Bone china; photographic transfer portrait, gilding. Royal Doulton, Burslem.

B188a-b **Cup and saucer commemorating the 1906 New Zealand International Exhibition of Art and Industry,** showing the Exhibition Buildings at Christchurch, **1906**
Cup: Height: 6cm
Saucer: Diameter: 14cm
Earthenware; transfer prints. Royal Doulton, Burslem.
Canterbury Museum Collection. EC188.370

B189 **Teapot with crackle glaze and frieze of kiwis, 1924-1940s. Made for John Bates & Co. Ltd. Christchurch, New Zealand**
Height: 13cm; width: 20cm
Earthenware; transfer print. Royal Doulton, Burslem.

B190a-b **Maori Art cup and saucer, white ground with red and black rafter pattern, c. 1925**
Cup: Height: 5.6cm; width:10.3 max.cm
Saucer: Diameter: 13.4cm
Bone china; transfer polychrome print, gilding. Royal Doulton, Burslem.
Otago Museum, Dunedin. F70.194; F70.196

B191 **Maori Art plate, white ground with red and black rafter pattern, c. 1925**
Diameter: 15.5cm
Bone china; transfer polychrome print, gilding. Royal Doulton, Burslem.
Otago Museum, Dunedin. F70.195

B192 **Maori Art teapot, yellow ground with red and black rafter pattern, c. 1925**
Bone china; transfer polychrome print, gilding. Royal Doulton, Burslem.
Auckland Museum. K6737.1/2

Burslem Doulton Character Jugs

B193 *Gone Away,* **1960-82**
Size: Small
Designer: **Garry Sharpe**

B194 *Gardener,* **1973-81**
Size: Small
Designer: **David Biggs**

B195 *Monty,* **1946-54**
Size: Large
Designer: **Harry Fenton**

B196 *'Ard of 'Earing,* **1964-67**
Size: Large
Designer: **David Biggs**

B197 *The McCallum,* Kingsware

B198 *Mr Pickwick,* **1938-48**
Odd size
Designer: **Leslie Harradine**

B199 *Sairey Gamp,* **1938-86**
Size: Small
Designer: **Leslie Harradine**
Grant & Ngaire Wright

B200 *Touchstone,* **1936-60**
Size: Large
Designer: **Charles Noke**

B201 *Dick Turpin* [first version], **1935-60**
Size: Large
Designers: **Charles Noke and Harry Fenton**

B202 *Merlin,* **1960-**
Size: Small
Designer: **Garry Sharpe**

B203 *Sleuth,* **1987, special colourway**
Size: Small
Designer: **Alan Moore**

B204 *Old Salt,* **1961-**
Size: Small
Designer: **Garry Sharpe**

B205 *John Barleycorn* [early version], **1934-9**
Size: Large
Designer: **Charles Noke**

B206 *Old Charley,* **1934-83**
Size: Large
Designer: **Charles Noke**

B207 *Granny* [early version], **1935-83**
Size: Large
Designer: **Harry Fenton**

B208 *'Owd Mac,* **1938-86**
Size: Small
Designer: **Harry Fenton**

B209 *Captain Hook,* **1965-71**
Size: Small
Designers: **Max Henk and David Biggs**

B210 **_Robin Hood_ [first version]**, 1947-60
Size: Large
Designer: **Harry Fenton**

B211 **_Cook & Cheshire Cat_**, 1990-
Size: Large
Designer: **William K. Harper**

B212 **_Mad Hatter_**, 1965-83
Size: Small
Designer: **Max Henk**

B213 **_Mephistopheles_, double-faced character jug**, 1937-48
Size: Large
Designers: **Charles Noke and Harry Fenton**

B214 **_The Clown_, (white-haired)**, 1951-55
Size: Large
Designer: **Harry Fenton**

B215 **_The Maori_ character jug**, 1939
Size: Large

All modelled, slip-cast. Royal Doulton, Burslem.

B216 **_Churchill_ loving cup. _Winston Spencer Churchill Prime Minister of Britain – 1940 – This Loving Cup Was Made During the "Battle of Britain" As A Tribute To A Great Leader. Modelled by Noke,_** 1940-1
Size: Large
Earthenware; ivory glaze, modelled and slip-cast. Royal Doulton, Burslem.
Museum of Applied Arts and Sciences, Sydney, Australia.

Lambeth Doulton Toby Jugs

L135 **_The Man on a Barrel_**, 1891-1902
Height: 31cm
Salt glaze stoneware; slip-cast. Doulton & Co., Lambeth.

L136 **_Toby XX_**, c. 1925
This jug has been specially marked for Ye Olde Cock Tavern, 22 Fleet Street, London.
Height: 16.5cm
Designer: **Harry Simeon**
Polychrome stoneware; slip-cast. Royal Doulton, Lambeth.

Burslem Doulton Toby Jugs

B217 **_The Huntsman_**, c. 1910
Designer: **Harry Fenton**
Height: 18cm
Kingsware, slip-cast with E.P.N.S. lid. Royal Doulton, Burslem.

B218 **_Charlie_**, 1918
Designer: **Unknown**
Height: 28cm
Earthenware; slip-cast. Royal Doulton, Burslem.

B219 **_Old Charley_**, 1939-60
Designer: **Harry Fenton**
Height: 22cm
Earthenware; slip-cast. Royal Doulton, Burslem.

B220 **_Winston Churchill_**, 1941-
Designer: **Harry Fenton**
Height: 16.5cm
Earthenware; slip-cast. Royal Doulton, Burslem.

Burslem Doulton Limited and Special Edition Jugs and Loving Cups

B221 **_Sir Francis Drake_ jug, issued in a limited edition of 500**, 1933
Height: 26.7cm
Designers: **Charles Noke and Harry Fenton**
Earthenware; low-relief modelling, slip-cast. Royal Doulton, Burslem.

B222 **_Jan Van Riebeeck_ loving cup, issued in a limited edition of 300**, 1952
Height: 26cm
Designers: **C. J. Noke and Harry Fenton**
Earthenware; slip-cast, low-relief modelling. Royal Doulton, Burslem.

B223 **_The Three Musketeers_ loving cup, issued in a limited edition of 1600**, 1936
Height: 26.7cm
Designers: **C. J. Noke and Harry Fenton**
Earthenware; slip-cast, low-relief modelling. Royal Doulton, Burslem.

B224 **_John Peel_ loving cup, issued in a limited edition of 500**, 1933
Height: 22.9cm
Unsigned
Earthenware; low-relief modelling, slip-cast. Royal Doulton, Burslem.

B225 **_William Shakespeare_ jug, issued in a limited edition of 1000**, 1933
Height: 26.3cm
Designer: **Charles Noke**
Earthenware; low-relief modelling, slip-cast. Royal Doulton, Burslem.

B226 **_The Pied Piper_ jug, issued in a limited edition of 600**, 1934
Height: 25.8cm
Designers: **Charles Noke and Harry Fenton**
Earthenware; low-relief modelling, slip-cast. Royal Doulton, Burslem.

Lambeth Doulton Animal Figurines

L137 **Duck, 1937**
Height: 46cm; width: 13.5cm; length: 30cm
Finial for washing line posts, for a St.Pancras Housing
Association estate.
Artist: **Gilbert Bayes**
Polychrome stoneware. Royal Doulton, Lambeth.
Dunedin Public Art Gallery.

L138 **Crow, c. *1937***
Height: 48.5cm; width: 12cm; length: 17cm
Finial for washing line posts, for a St.Pancras Housing
Association estate.
Artist: **Gilbert Bayes**
Polychrome stoneware. Royal Doulton, Lambeth.
Dunedin Public Art Gallery.

L139 **Lizard, c. 1912-20s**
Height: 3.2cm; width: 6.8cm; length: 12cm
Stoneware; slip-cast. Royal Doulton, Lambeth.

L140 **Lizard on a rock**
Height: 13cm
Artist: **Mark V. Marshall**
Stoneware; salt-glazed, modelled. Doulton, Lambeth.
Sir Henry Doulton Gallery, Royal Doulton (U.K.) Ltd.

L141 **Dragon on a grotto, 1902-12**
Height: 27.3cm; width: 15.4cm; length: 11.5cm
Artist: **Mark V. Marshall**
Stoneware; salt-glazed, modelled. Doulton, Lambeth.
Museum of Applied Arts and Sciences, Sydney, Australia.
A3857

Burslem Doulton Animal Figurines

B227 **Brown fox, H.N.130, 1920**
Height: 22cm; width: 13.5cm; length: 21.5cm
Bone china; slip-cast, hand-painted. Royal Doulton,
Burslem.

B228 **Fox in Red Hunting Coat H.N.100, 1939 mould**
Height: 15.5cm; diameter: 11cm
Bone china; slip-cast, hand-painted. Royal Doulton,
Burslem.

B229 **Seated cat, red glaze, 1902-13**
Height: 13.5cm; width: 5cm; length: 7cm
Earthenware; slip-cast, hand-painted. Royal Doulton,
Burslem.

B230 **Butterfly, *Camberwell Beauty,* c. 1928-39**
Width: 6cm; length: 10cm
Bone china; slip-cast, hand-painted. Royal Doulton,
Burslem.

B231 **Sleeping Calf H.N.1161, 1937 mould**
Height: 6cm; width: 9cm; length: 14.5cm
Artist: **Raoh Schorr**
Earthenware; slip-cast, matt white glaze. Royal Doulton,
Burslem.

B232 **Baboon H.N.140, mould 147, 1917**
Height: 15cm; width: 12.5cm; length: 14cm
Bone china; slip-cast, hand-painted. Royal Doulton,
Burslem.

B233 **Sleeping Piglet H.N.2651**
Height: 2.7cm; width: 3.8cm; length: 6.5cm
Bone china; slip-cast, hand-painted. Royal Doulton,
Burslem.

B234 ***Old Bill* H.N.146 – bull dog with steel helmet and
haversack, c. 1916**
Height: 16.5cm; length: 21cm
Earthenware; slip-cast, hand-painted. Royal Doulton,
Burslem.

B235 **Matchstriker and holder in form of a double-head
bulldog draped with Union Jack. Rd.No. 648,328,
c. 1911**
Height: 8cm; width: 14.8cm; length: 19cm
Earthenware; slip-cast, hand-painted. Royal Doulton,
Burslem.

B236 **Rough haired terrier, Champion *Crackley Starter*,
H.N.1007**
Height: 19cm; width: 6.5cm; length: 28cm
Bone china; slip-cast, hand-painted. Royal Doulton,
Burslem.

B237 **Flambé seated bulldog, c. 1920**
Height: 13.6cm; width: 11.2cm; length: 18cm
Earthenware; slip-cast, transmutation glaze. Royal
Doulton, Burslem.

B238 **Flambé collie**
Height: 18.2cm; width: 10.9cm; length: 11.5cm
Earthenware; slip-cast, transmutation glaze. Royal
Doulton, Burslem.

B239 **Flambé goat, *Capricorn***
Height: 25.7cm; width: 13.3cm; length: 10.2cm
Earthenware; slip-cast, transmutation glaze. Royal
Doulton, Burslem.

B240 **Flambé pig with silver rim**
Height: 5.4cm; length: 11.3cm; width: 6.8cm
Earthenware; slip-cast, transmutation glaze. Royal
Doulton, Burslem.

B241 **Pair of Flambé embracing apes**
Height: 13cm
Possibly from a design by Leslie Harradine.
Earthenware; slip-cast, transmutation glaze. Royal
Doulton, Burslem.

B242 **Flambé tiger, 1932-6**
Height: 15cm; width: 10.3cm; length: 35.5cm
Earthenware; slip-cast, transmutation glaze. Royal
Doulton, Burslem.

B243 **Sung glaze elephant, 1930s**
Height: 31.5cm; length: 50cm
Signed: **Noke and Fred Allen**
Earthenware; slip-cast, transmutation glaze. Royal
Doulton, Burslem.

B244 **Flambé trout, 1930s**
Height: 6.2cm; width: 7.5cm; length: 15cm
Earthenware; slip-cast, transmutation glaze. Royal
Doulton, Burslem.
Museum of Applied Arts and Sciences, Sydney, Australia.
A1501

Lambeth Doulton Figurines

L142 **Garden statue, woman with flowers, probably representing *Flora*, 1902-23 (Probably modelled in the 1890s)**
Height: 130cm; width: 40cm
Designer: **Unknown, but possibly John Broad**
Terracotta. Royal Doulton, Lambeth.

L143 *Diana,* **c. 1880**
Height: 29.7cm; diameter: 9.7 max.cm
Artist: **John Broad (attributed)**
Terracotta. Doulton & Co., Lambeth.
Museum of Applied Arts and Sciences, Sydney, Australia. 2824

L144 *Sairey Gamp,* **c. 1913**
Height: 19.8cm; width: 10.5cm; length: 11.5cm

L145 *Mr Pecksniff* **H21, c. 1913**
Height: 23cm; width: 8.5cm; length: 6.5cm

L146 *Mr Squeers,* **c. 1913**
Height: 23.5cm

L147 *Mr Pickwick* **H19, c. 1913**
Height: 22cm; width: 9cm; length: 10.8cm
Artist: **Leslie Harradine**
Slip-cast stoneware. Royal Doulton, Lambeth.

L148 *Charles Dickens,* **1912**
Height: 16cm; width: 12cm; length: 12cm
Artist: **Leslie Harradine**
Slip-cast stoneware. Royal Doulton, Lambeth.

L149 *Organist,* **Merry Musicians series, 1902-1913**
Height: 13.4cm; diameter: 8cm
Artist: **George Tinworth**
Salt-glazed stoneware. Royal Doulton, Lambeth.
Museum of Applied Arts and Sciences, Sydney, Australia. A3818

L150 *Tambourine Player,* **Merry Musicians series, 1902-1913**
Height: 10.8cm
Artist: **George Tinworth**
Salt-glazed stoneware. Royal Doulton, Lambeth.
Auckland Museum. C1757

L151 *The Toiler,* **c. 1907**
Height: 21.6cm
Artist: **Leslie Harradine**
Stoneware; slip-cast.
Royal Doulton, Lambeth.

L152 **Spirit flask depicting British politician, Lord Haldane, c. 1908-11**
Height: 19.7cm
Artist: **Leslie Harradine**
Stoneware; salt-glazed, slip-cast. Royal Doulton, Lambeth.
O'Neill Collection.

L154 *Boer War Soldier,* **c. 1900**
Height: 32cm
Artist: **John Broad**
Stoneware; salt-glazed. Doulton & Co., Lambeth.
Sir Henry Doulton Gallery, Royal Doulton (UK) Ltd.

L155 *Mother and Child* **H24, c. 1912-14.**
Height: 23cm; width: 8cm; length: 7cm
Artist: **Leslie Harradine**
Stoneware; slip-cast. Royal Doulton, Lambeth.

Burslem Doulton Figurines

B245 *Marriage of Art and Industry* **H.N.2261, 1958**
A limited edition of 12, created especially for the Brussels International Exhibition of 1958.
Designer: **Margaret May (Peggy) Davies**
Slip-cast, hand-painted. Royal Doulton, Burslem.
Sir Henry Doulton Gallery, Royal Doulton (U.K.) Ltd.

B246 *Lady with Rose* **H.N.48A, 1916-38**
Artist: **E. W. Light**

B247 *Milkmaid* **(also known as *Shepherdess*) H.N.735, 1925-1938**

B248 *Phyllis* **H.N.1698, 1935-49**
Artist: **Leslie Harradine**

B249 *Pretty Lady* **H.N.565, 1923-38**
Artist: **Harry Tittensor**

B250-1 *The Chelsea Pair (Female)* **H.N.577, 1923-1938, *The Chelsea Pair (Male)* H.N.579, 1923-38**
Artist: **Leslie Harradine**

B252a-b *Patricia* **(miniature) M7, 1932-45, *The Paisley Shawl* (miniature) M4, 1932-45**
Artist: **Leslie Harradine**

B253 *The Gossips* **H.N.1426, 1930-49**
Artist: **Leslie Harradine**

B254 *Sonia* **H.N.1738, 1935-49**
Artist: **Leslie Harradine**

B255 *Top o' the Hill* **H.N.1833, 1937-71**
Artist: **Leslie Harradine**

B256 *Top o' the Hill* **H.N.1834, 1937-**
Mrs K. A. Farr.

B257 *Top o' the Hill* **H.N.1849, 1938-75**
Laurie Trubshoe.

B258 *Top o' the Hill.* **Australian Bicentennial edition, 1988**

B259 *Top o' the Hill* **(miniature). Royal Doulton International Collectors' Club special issue.**

B260 *Dreamland* **H.N.1473, 1931-38**
Artist: **Leslie Harradine**

B261 *The Bather* **(first version, model 428) H.N.687, 1924-1949**
Artist: **Leslie Harradine**

B262 **Butterfly** H.N.719, 1925-38
    Artist: **Leslie Harradine**

B263 **Angela** H.N.1204, 1926-38
    Artist: **Leslie Harradine**

B264 **Lido Lady** H.N.1220, 1927-38
    Artist: **Leslie Harradine**

B265 **Gladys** H.N.1740
    Artist: **Leslie Harradine**

B266 **Gloria** H.N.1700, 1935-38
    Artist: **Leslie Harradine**

B267 **Clothilde** H.N.1598, 1933-49
    Artist: **Leslie Harradine**

B268 **Pensive Moments** H.N.2704, 1975-81
    Artist: **Peggy Davies**
    Laurie Trubshoe.

B269 **Fragrance** H.N.2334, 1966-
    Artist: **Peggy Davies**
    Laurie Trubshoe.

B270 **Awakening** H.N.2837, 1981-
    Artist: **Peggy Davies**
    J. & J. Jackson.

B271 **Sweet Perfume** H.N.3094, 1986-
    Artist: **Pauline Parsons**

B272 **The Orange Lady** H.N.1759, 1936-75
    Artist: **Leslie Harradine**
    Mrs K. M. Slow.

B273 **Mask Seller** H.N.2103, 1953-
    Artist: **Leslie Harradine**

B274 **Romany Sue** H.N.1758, 1936-49
    Artist: **Leslie Harradine**

B275 **Tuppence a Bag** H.N.2230, 1968-
    Artist: **Mary Nicoll**
    J. & J. Jackson.

B276 **Madonna of the Square** H.N.10, 1913-38
    Artist: **Phoebe Stabler, R.A.**

B277 **The Balloon Seller** H.N.583, 1923-49
    Artist: **Leslie Harradine**

B278 **Yardley's Old English Lavender** advertising model, c. 1924
    Artist: **(probably) Leslie Harradine**

B279 **Old Balloon Seller** H.N.1315, 1929-
(early version).
    Artist: **Leslie Harradine**
    J. & J. Jackson.

B280 **The Balloon Man** H.N.1954, 1940-
(early version)
    Artist: **Leslie Harradine**
    J. & J. Jackson.

B281 **Abdullah** H.N.1410, 1930-38
    Artist: **Leslie Harradine**

B282 **An Orange Vendor**, c. 1917
This figure does not have an H.N. number, and may be a pilot version of H.N.72, issued 1917-38.
    Artist: **Charles Noke**

B283 **The Mendicant** H.N.1365, 1929-69
    Artist: **Leslie Harradine**
    Winifred Swires Bequest, Canterbury Museum Collection.

B284 **An Arab** H.N.33, 1913-38 (1919 mould date)
    Artist: **Charles Noke**

B285 **The Emir** H.N.1604, 1933-49
    Artist: **Charles Noke**

B286 **The Carpet Seller** H.N.1493, 1932 - (early version)
    Artist: **Charles Noke**

B287 **West Wind** H.N.1776. Introduced in 1933 as a limited edition of 25, and sold out by **1939**.
    Artist: **Richard Garbe, R.A.**
    Museum of New Zealand Te Papa Tongarewa.

B288 **Spirit of the Wind** H.N.1777. Introduced in 1993 as a limited edition of 50, and sold out by **1939**.
    Artist: **Richard Garbe, R.A.**
    Museum of New Zealand Te Papa Tongarewa.

B289-290
    Darby H.N.2024, and **Joan** H.N.2023, 1949-59
    Artist: **Leslie Harradine**

    Tolkien Series – The Lord of the Rings, 1980-4
    Artist: **David Lyttleton**
B291 **Frodo** H.N.2912
B292 **Gollum** H.N.2913
B293 **Gandalf** H.N.2911
B294 **Samwise** H.N.2925
B295 **Tom Bombadil** H.N.2924

B296 **Sam Weller**
B297 **Stiggins**
B298 **Alfred Jingle**
B299 **Dick Swiveller**
B300 **Mr Pickwick**
B301 **Serjeant Buzfuz**
B302 **Mrs Bardell**
B303 **Tony Weller**
B304 **The Fat Boy**
B305 **Captain Cuttle**
B306 **Little Nell**
B307 **Trotty Veck**
B308 **Artful Dodger**
B309 **Fagin**
B310 **Bill Sikes**
B311 **Oliver Twist**
B312 **Bumble**
B313 **Uriah Heep**
B314 **David Copperfield**
B315 **Mr Micawber**
B316 **Scrooge**
B317 **Tiny Tim**

    Artist: **Leslie Harradine**
    Bone china; slip-cast. Royal Doulton, Burslem.

B318   **Shakespeare**, c. 1893
       Canterbury Museum Collection.
B319   **Lily Langtry or Sarah Bernhardt as *Cleopatra*, c. 1893**
       (One of only two known copies)
B320   **Ellen Terry as *Queen Catherine*, c. 1893**
B321   **Sir Henry Irving as *Cardinal Wolsey*, c. 1893**
B322   *Marguerite/Mephistopheles from Faust*, c. 1893
       City Museum & Art Gallery, Stoke-on-Trent, England.

       Artist: **Charles Noke**
       Parian-type bodies with vellum glaze, hand-colouring,
       gilding by Robert Allen's studio. Doulton & Co., Burslem.

B323   *Captain MacHeath* **H.N.464** from *The Beggars Opera*,
       1921-1949
B324   *Polly Peachum* **H.N.465** from *The Beggars Opera*, **1921-
       49**
       Artist: **Leslie Harradine** after **Claud Lovatt Fraser**

B325   *Pierrette* **H.N.644 (first version, model 445), 1924-1938**
       Artist: **Leslie Harradine**

B326   *The Sentimental Pierrot* **H.N.36, 1914-38**
       Artist: **Charles Noke**

B327   *Elsie Maynard* **H.N.639** from *Yeoman of the Guard,* **1924-
       1949**
       Artist: **Charles Noke**

B328   *Henry Lytton as Jack Point* **H.N.610** from *Yeoman of
       the Guard,* **1924-49**
       Artist: **Charles Noke**
       Sir Henry Doulton Gallery, Royal Doulton (UK) Ltd.

B329   *One of the Forty* **H.N.480 (first version), 1921-38**
       Artist: **Harry Tittensor**
       Sir Henry Doulton Gallery, Royal Doulton (UK) Ltd.

B330   *Kate Hardcastle* **H.N.1718, 1935-49**
       Artist: **Leslie Harradine**

B331   *Salome* **H.N.1775,** issued in **1933** as a limited edition of
       100, and sold out by **1939**
       Artist: **Richard Garbe**
       Museum of Applied Arts and Sciences, Sydney, Australia.

B332   *Doris Keane as Cavallini* **H.N.90 (first version, model
       205), 1918-36**
       Artist: **Charles Noke**

B333   **[W. S. Penley as]** *Charley's Aunt.* This version has no
       H.N. number and was probably a special order of H.N.35,
       c. 1913-18
       Artist: **Albert Toft**

B334   *A Jester* **H.N.55, 1916-38**
       Artist: **Charles Noke**

B335   *Lord Olivier as Richard III* **N.H.2881,** issued as a
       limited edition of 750 in **1985**
       Artist: **Eric Griffiths**

B336   *Jack Point* **H.N.2080** from *Yeomen of the Guard,* **1952-**
       Artist: **Charles Noke**

B337   *Moorish Minstrel*, c. 1892
       Parian-type body; vellum glaze. Doulton & Co., Burslem.

B338   *Moorish Piper Minstrel* **H.N.416, 1920-38**
       Artist: **Charles Noke**
       Royal Doulton, Burslem.

B339-350   *Dulcimer* **H.N.2798**
           Viola d'Amore **H.N.2797**
           Hurdy Gurdy **H.N.2796**
           French Horn **H.N.2795**
           Virginals **H.N.2427**
           Chitarrone **H.N.2700**
           Cymbals **H.N.2699**
           Harp **H.N.2482**
           Flute **H.N.2483**
           Violin **H.N.2432**
           Lute **H.N.2431**
           Cello **H.N.2331**

       Lady Musicians series, issued as a limited edition of 750
       between **1970** and **1976**, and sold out.
       Artist: **Peggy Davies**
       Bone china; slip-cast, hand-painted. Royal Doulton,
       Burslem.

B351   *Giselle* **H.N.2139, 1954-69**
B352   *Giselle, Forest Glade* **H.N.2140, 1954-65**
       Artist: **Peggy Davies**
       Bone china; slip-cast, hand-painted. Royal Doulton,
       Burslem.

B353   *Polish Dancer* **H.N.2836,** introduced as part of the
       limited (750) edition series *Dancers of the World* in **1980**.
       Artist: **Peggy Davies**
       Bone china; slip-cast, hand-painted. Royal Doulton,
       Burslem.
       J. & J. Jackson.

B354   *Fisherwomen.* This has no H.N. number but is clearly
       related to a design for H.N.80. It is the second only
       known example and is a unique colourway, **c. 1918**
       Artist: **Charles Noke**
       Earthenware; slip-cast, hand-painted. Royal Doulton,
       Burslem.

B355   *Young Mother with Child* **H.N.1301, 1928-38**
       To date this is the only recorded example of the design.
       Artist: **Unknown**
       Earthenware; slip-cast, hand-painted. Royal Doulton,
       Burslem.

B356   *Lady with Large Hat* **H.N.46 No. 3 (also known as *The
       Gainsborough Hat*), 1915-38**
       Artist: **Harry Tittensor**
       Bone china; slip-cast, hand-painted. Royal Doulton,
       Burslem.

B357-360   **The Gainsborough Ladies Series (current)**
           Isabella, Countess of Sefton
           Mary, Countess Howe
           The Hon. Frances Duncombe
           Sophia Charlotte, Lady Sheffield.
           Artist: **Peter Gee**
           Bone china; slip-cast, hand-painted. Royal Doulton,
           Burslem.

B361-364   *Les Saisons.* **Limited edition series, 1987-9**
Printemps **H.N.3066**
Eté **H.N.3067**
Automne **H.N.3068**
Hiver **H.N.3069**
Artist: **Robert Jefferson**
Bone china; slip-cast, hand-painted. Royal Doulton, Burslem.

B365   *Taking Things Easy* **H.N.2677, 1975-87**
Artist: **Mary Nicoll**
Bone china; slip-cast, hand-painted. Royal Doulton, Burslem.

B366   *The Cup of Tea* **H.N.2322, 1964-83**
Artist: **Mary Nicoll**
Bone china; slip-cast, hand-painted. Royal Doulton, Burslem.
J. & J. Jackson.

B367   *The Favourite* **H.N.2249, 1960-**
Artist: **Mary Nicoll**
Bone china; slip-cast, hand-painted. Royal Doulton, Burslem.
J. & J. Jackson.

B368   *Lunchtime* **H.N.2485, 1973-81**
Artist: **Mary Nicoll**
Bone china; slip-cast, hand-painted. Royal Doulton, Burslem.
J.& J. Jackson.

B369   *The Welsh Girl* **H.N.39, 1914-38**
Artist: **E. W. Light**
Earthenware; slip-cast, hand-painted. Royal Doulton, Burslem.
Sir Henry Doulton Gallery, Royal Doulton (UK) Ltd.

B370   *Fortune Teller* **H.N.2159, 1955-67**
Artist: **Leslie Harradine**
Bone china; slip-cast, hand-painted. Royal Doulton, Burslem.

B371   *The Apple Maid* **H.N.2160, 1957-62**
Artist: **Leslie Harradine**
Bone china; slip-cast, hand-painted. Royal Doulton, Burslem.

B372   *The Boatman* **H.N.2417, 1971-87**
Artist: **Mary Nicoll**
Bone china; slip-cast, hand-painted. Royal Doulton, Burslem.

B373   *The Lobster Man* **H.N.2317, 1964-**
Artist: **Mary Nicoll**
Bone china; slip-cast, hand-painted. Royal Doulton, Burslem.
J. & J. Jackson.

B374   *The Shepherd* **H.N.1975 (fourth version, model 1190), 1945-75**
Artist: **Harry Fenton**
Bone china; slip-cast, hand-painted. Royal Doulton, Burslem.

B375   *The Wayfarer* **H.N.2362, 1970-76**
Artist: **Mary Nicoll**
Bone china; slip-cast, hand-painted. Royal Doulton, Burslem.

B376   *Oh! Law!,* **c. 1893**
Artist: **Charles Noke**
Parian-type body; vellum glaze. Doulton & Co., Burslem.
Alexander Turnbull Library.

B377   *The Judge* **H.N.2443, 1972-76**
Artist: **Mary Nicoll**
Bone china; slip-cast, hand-painted. Royal Doulton, Burslem.

B378   *In the Stocks* **H.N.2163 (second version, model 1502), 1955-59**
Artist: **Mary Nicoll**
Bone china; slip-cast, hand-painted. Royal Doulton, Burslem.

B379   *Votes for Women* **H.N.2816, 1978-82**
Artist: **William K. Harper**
Bone china; slip-cast, hand-painted. Royal Doulton, Burslem.
J. & J. Jackson.

B380   *King Charles* **H.N.2084, 1952-92**
Artists: **Charles Noke and Harry Tittensor**
Bone china; slip-cast, hand-painted. Royal Doulton, Burslem.

B381   *Guy Fawkes* **H.N.98, 1918-49**
Artist: **Charles Noke**
Bone china; slip-cast, hand-painted. Royal Doulton, Burslem.

B382-385 **Four figures from Famous English Women series:**
Matilda **H.N.2011, 1948-53**
Sir Henry Doulton Gallery, Royal Doulton (UK) Ltd.
Eleanor of Provence **H.N.2009, 1948-53**
Philippa of Hainault **H.N.200, 1948-53**
Sir Henry Doulton Gallery, Royal Doulton (UK) Ltd.
The Lady Ann Nevill **H.N.2006, 1948-53**
Artist: **Peggy Davies**
Bone china; slip-cast, hand-painted. Royal Doulton, Burslem.

B386   *Queen Elizabeth the Queen Mother as the Duchess of York* **H.N.3230, 1989-**
Artist: **Pauline Parsons**
Bone china; slip-cast, hand-painted. Royal Doulton, Burslem.

B387   *Digger (New Zealand)* **H.N.321, 1918-38**
Artist: **Ernest W. Light**
Bone china; slip-cast, hand-painted. Royal Doulton, Burslem.

B388   *Digger (Australia)* **H.N.322, 1918-38**
Artist: **Ernest W. Light**
Bone china; slip-cast, hand-painted. Royal Doulton, Burslem.

B389   *Blighty* **H.N.323, 1918-38**
Artist: **Ernest W. Light**
Bone china; slip-cast, Titanian glaze (green) Royal Doulton, Burslem.

B390   *The Alchemist* **H.N.1282, 1928-38**
Artist: **Leslie Harradine**
Bone china; slip-cast, hand-painted. Royal Doulton, Burslem.

B391 **A Spook H.N.50, 1916-38**
Artist: **Harry Tittensor**
Bone china; slip-cast, hand-painted. Royal Doulton, Burslem.
Sir Henry Doulton Gallery, Royal Doulton (UK) Ltd.

B392 **Blue Beard H.N.1528 (second version, model 745), 1932-49**
Artist: **Leslie Harradine**
Bone china; slip-cast, hand-painted. Royal Doulton, Burslem.

B393 **The Genie H.N.2989, 1983-**
Artist: **Robert Tabbenor**
Bone china; slip-cast, hand-painted. Royal Doulton, Burslem.

B394 **The Goosegirl, c. 1921-38**
This bone china version has lost its H.N. number, but is similar to H.N.437 (earthenware).
Artist: **Leslie Harradine**
Bone china; slip-cast, hand-painted. Royal Doulton, Burslem.

B395 **The Pied Piper H.N.2102, 1953-76**
Artist: **Leslie Harradine**
Bone china; slip-cast, hand-painted. Royal Doulton, Burslem.

B396 **Daffy Down Dilly H.N.1712, 1935-75**
Artist: **Unknown**
Bone china; slip-cast, hand-painted. Royal Doulton, Burslem.

B397 **St George H.N.2067, 1950-76**
Artist: **Stanley Thorogood A.R.C.A.**
Bone china; slip-cast, hand-painted. Royal Doulton, Burslem.
J. & J. Jackson.

B398 **Darling H.N.1 (first version, model 89). Mould stamped for June 1919**
Artist: **Charles Vyse**
Bone china; slip-cast, hand-painted. Royal Doulton, Burslem.

B399 **This Little Pig H.N.1793, 1936-**
Artist: **Leslie Harradine**
Bone china; slip-cast, hand-painted. Royal Doulton, Burslem.

B400 **Candlestick in form of a Girl on a Crab, 1891-1901**
Artist: Unknown
Parian-type body; vellum glaze, tinted. Doulton & Co., Burslem.

B401 **Sleep H.N.24 No. 264, 1913-23 (Withdrawn 1938)**
Artist: **Phoebe Stabler**
Bone china; slip-cast, hand-painted. Royal Doulton, Burslem.

B402 **The Coquette H.N.20, 1913-38**
Artist: **William White**
Bone china; slip-cast, hand-painted. Royal Doulton, Burslem.

B403 **The Diligent Scholar H.N.26, 1913-38**
Artist: **William White**
Bone china; slip-cast, hand-painted. Royal Doulton, Burslem.

B404 **The Sleepy Scholar (early version of H.N.16), c. 1913**
Artist: **William White**
Bone china; slip-cast, hand-painted. Royal Doulton, Burslem.

B405 **The Sleepy Scholar H.N.16, 1913-38**
Artist: **William White**
Bone china; slip-cast, hand-painted. Royal Doulton, Burslem.

B406 **A Child from Williamsburg H.N.2154, 1964-**
Bone china; slip-cast, hand-painted. Royal Doulton, Burslem.

B407 **Boy from Williamsburg H.N.2183, 1969-**
Artist: **Peggy Davies**
Bone china; slip-cast, hand-painted. Royal Doulton, Burslem.
Laurie Trubshoe.

B408 **Baby Bunting H.N.2108, 1953-9**
Artist: **Peggy Davies**
Bone china; slip-cast, hand-painted. Royal Doulton, Burslem.

B409 **Wee Willie Winkie H.N.2050, 1953-59**
Artist: **Peggy Davies**
Bone china; slip-cast, hand-painted. Royal Doulton, Burslem.

B410 **Little Boy Blue H.N.2062, 1950-73**
Artist: **Leslie Harradine**
Bone china; slip-cast, hand-painted. Royal Doulton, Burslem.

B411 **Jack H.N.2060, 1950-71**
Artist: **Leslie Harradine**
Bone china; slip-cast, hand-painted. Royal Doulton, Burslem.

B412 **Jill H.N.2061, 1950-71**
Artist: **Leslie Harradine**
Bone china; slip-cast, hand-painted. Royal Doulton, Burslem.

Burslem Doulton Series Ware

Blue Children:
B413 Vase, scene of small child holding a balloon.
B414 Pilgrim flask, gilt tracery and scenes of a woman by the seashore, and a woman and child in a garden.
B415 Vase with two small girls sheltering from snow under an umbrella.
B416 Vase with handles, scene of two boys talking.
B417 Vase, scene of boy and girl peeping into a hole in a tree-trunk.
B418 Wall plate, two young girls seated under a tree.
B419 Jardinière, scene of little girl with her doll, talking to a frog.
B420 Jardinière, scene of a woman and small child in a snowy rural landscape.
B421 Vase, scene of four children playing Blind Man's Bluff.
B422 Ewer vase, scene of seated woman playing a guitar.

B423   Vase, girl giving a small boy a piggy-back ride.

B424   Jardinière, scene of three small girls watching Tinkerbell.

Dickensware:

B425   Shaving mug – *Sam Weller*

B426   Hatpin holder – *Old Pegotty*

B427   Sugar sifter – *Sairey Gamp*

B428   Miniature vase – *The Artful Dodger*

B429   Milk jug – *Alfred Jingles*

B430   Jug – *Mr Pecksniff*

B431   Stein – *Mr Toots*

B432   Vase (shape 7391) – *Mr Dodson*

B433   Ewer – *Mark Tapley*

B434   Cake plate – *Sidney Carton*

B435   Vase – *Barnaby Rudge*

B436   Rack plate – *Mrs Bardell*

B437   Rack plate – *Trotty Veck*
    Canterbury Museum Collection

B438   Vase – *Mr Chadband*

B439   Vase (7383) – *Mr Micawber*

B440   Fruit dish (Leeds) – *Mr Mantalini*

B441   Fluted plate – *Captain Cuttle*

B442   Cheese dish (Canute) – The Fat Boy. Also has **Barkis**, and **Poor Jo**

B443   Candlestick (7227) – *Bill Sikes* [misspelt Sykes]

B444   Vase – *Poor Jo*

B445   Stein – *Little Nell*

B446   Teapot stand with E.P.N.S. rim – *Fagin*

B447   Bread plate – *Serjeant Buzfuz*

B448   Biscuit barrel (Margot) – *Mr Squeers*

B449   Pair of salad servers, E.P.N.S. – (fork) *Mr Pickwick*, (spoon) *Tony Weller*

Assorted Series Wares (rack plates)

B450   *Bayeux Tapestry – Spying the Comet – Isti mirant stella*, **1907-30**

B451   *King Arthur's Knights* or *Tournament*, **1908-30**

B452   *Vikings* (Series B), **1912-28**

B453   *Ye Queen of Hearts we all do know*
    She won our hearts long years ago
    Playing card characters designed in 1909 by Augustus L. Jansson, an American painter, **1913-32**

B454   *Witches*, **1906-28**

B455   *Sampler* or *Peter Pan*, house with cows in foreground, **1924-36**

B456   *Home Waters*, unloading the sailboat *Polly*. Designer: W. E. Grace, **1954-67**

B457   *Japanese Orbs*, Titanian glaze, **1921-40**

B458   *Gaffers*, old English yokel with a stick. Designer: Charles Noke, **1921-49**

B459   *Hunting – Morland*, galloping huntsman with whip aloft. (After designs by George Morland 1763-1804), **1901-28**

B460   *Old Moreton Hall*, the Squire taking Queen Elizabeth's hand, **1915-33**

B461   *The Professionals – Jester*, **1909-75**

B462   *Gibson Girl head.* (After **Charles Dana Gibson**, popular American satirist and illustrator.) **1901 – ?**

B463   *A Widow and her Friends.* (After **Charles Dana Gibson**.) **1901- ?**

B464   *HMS Lion 1914-18*, **c. 1918-20**

Assorted Series Wares

B465   Slop bowl, *Kateroo* cats by **David Henry Souter**, Australian illustrator, **1905-39**

B466   Rack plate *Kateroo* scene – *The Lovers*, **1905-39**

B467   Coffee pot, Sir Roger de Coverley – *Mr William with a young maid in the garden*, **1911-49**

B468   Coffee cup saucer, Sir Roger de Coverley – *Sir Roger on his feet*

B469   Coffee cup, Sir Roger de Coverley – *The Captain and the Widow*

B470   Oval vase, Cricketers – The All Black Team. *Good for Fifty*, **1906-30**

B471   Plate, Cricketers – The All Black Team. *Ready for Chances*, **1907**
    Judith Gilmore.

B472   Bread plate, Cricketers – The All Black Team. *There's Style*, **1915**
    Judith Gilmore.

B473   Vase, Cricketers – The All Black Team. *Next Man In*

B474   Sugar basin, W. S. Cooper Nursery Rhymes – *There was a little man*, **1903-39**

B475   Milk jug, W. S. Cooper Nursery Rhymes – *Old Mother Hubbard*
    M.H.Lum.

B476   Cup, Cricketers – The All Black Team. *Out for a Duck*, **1906-30**
    Judith Gilmore.

B477   Saucer, Cricketers – The All Black Team. *I wasn't ready*, **1908**
    Judith Gilmore.

B478   Cup/bowl, Cricketers – The All Black Team. *The Boss*, **1906-30**
    Judith Gilmore.

B479   Miniature honey pot, W. S. Cooper Nursery Rhymes – *Hey Diddle Diddle*

B480   Teapot, W. S. Cooper Nursery Rhymes – *There was an Old Woman who Lived in a Shoe*
    M. H. Lum.

B481a-c   Cup, saucer and plate, W. S. Cooper Nursery Rhymes – *To market, to market, to buy a fat pig...*
    M. H. Lum.

B482   Dutch candlestick, *Orlando* – Shakespeare series G, **1912-28**

B483   Matchbox holder-ashtray, *Falstaff*- Shakespeare series G, **1912-28**

B484   Hat pin holder, *Juliet* – Shakespeare series G, **1912-1928**

B485   Hair tidy, *Anne Page* – Shakespeare series G, **1912-1928**

B486   Sandwich tray (York), Falconry series, **1913-30**

B487   Biscuit barrel with E.P.N.S. lid and handle, Coaching Days series, innkeeper talking to passengers. Designer: Victor Venner, **1905-55**

B488   Rack plate *Ali Baba and the Treasure*, Arabian Nights series, **1909-28**

B489   Rack plate, *Ali Baba's Return*, Arabian Nights series, **1909-28**

B490   Tobacco jar, *Ali Baba at the cave "Open Sesame"*, Arabian Nights series, **1909-28**

B491   Rack plate, *Under the Greenwood Tree*, Under the Greenwood Tree (Robin Hood), **1912-67**

B492   Jug (Newlyn), *Robin Hood, Friend of the Poor*, Under the Greenwood Tree (Robin Hood), **1912-67**

B493-5 **Chamberpot, basin and ewer,** *Watchman, What of the Night*, **Nightwatchman series**
Designer: **Charles Noke, 1899-1945**

B496 **Rack plate,** *Give losers to speak and winners to laugh*, **Golf series**
Designer: **Charles Crombie, 1911-32**

B497 **Fluted dish,** *He hath good judgment who relieth not wholly on his own*, **Golf series**
Designer: **Charles Crombie, 1911-32**

B498 **Jardinière,** *Every dog has his day and every man his hour; He that always complains is never pitied*, **Golf series**
Designer: **Charles Crombie, 1911-32**

B499 **Jug (Tudor),** *The Compleat Angler*, **Gallant Fishers (Izaak Walton) B series, 1906 – ?**

B500 **Teapot (Joan), Gnomes series (B),** tree trunk with three gnomes among roots.
Designer: **Charles Noke** inspired by Arthur Rackham, **1927-50**

B501 **Sugar basin (Joan), Gnomes series (B),** tree trunk with gnomes behind mushrooms and among tree roots.
Designer: **Charles Noke** inspired by Arthur Rackham, **1927-50**

B502 **Jug (Westcott), Gnomes series (B),** tree trunk with five gnomes amongst tree roots.
Designer: **Charles Noke** inspired by Arthur Rackham, **1927-50**

B503 **Cake plate, Gnomes series (B),** tree trunk with six gnomes amongst tree roots.
Designer: **Charles Noke** inspired by Arthur Rackham, **1927-50**

B504 **Biscuit barrel, Skating series,** two skaters chasing each other, **1907-28**

B505 **Plaque,** *Harvest*, **Brangwyn Ware, 1931**

B506 **Jug,** *Harvest*, **Brangwyn Ware, 1930s**
Auckland Museum.

Bunnykins:

B507 **Saucer,** *Artist*. **Barbara Vernon, 1937-52**

B508 **Baby plate,** *Proposal*. **Barbara Vernon, 1937-67**

B509 **Plate,** *Feeding the Baby*. **Barbara Vernon, 1943 (1937-1967)**

B510 **Plate,** *Xmas Menu*. **Barbara Vernon, 1940-52**

B511 **Baby plate,** *Letterbox*. **Walter Hayward** after **Barbara Vernon, 1952- ?**

B512 **Bread plate,** *Family Photograph*. **Walter Hayward, 1954-70**

B513 **Rim fruit saucer,** *Toast for Tea Today*. **Walter Hayward, 1954-67**

B514 **Oval baby plate,** *Family Cycling*. **Walter Hayward, 1952-70**

B515 *Collector Bunnykins*. **A Royal Doulton International Collectors Club special issue. David Lyttleton, 1986**

B516 *Bedtime Bunnykins* **DB55, 1986**

B517 *Busy Needles* **DB10, 1974**

B518 *Be Prepared* **DB56, 1986**

B519 *Brownie Bunnykins* **DB61, 1987**

B520 *Jogging Bunnykins* **DB22, 1982**

B521 *Ace Bunnykins* **DB42, 1985**

B522 *Bogey Bunnykins*